The Ordination
of Women
to the Priesthood

THE SYNOD DEBATE
11 November 1992

The Verbatim Record

CHURCH HOUSE PUBLISHING
Church House, Great Smith Street, London SW1P 3NZ

ISBN 0 7151 3751 4

Published 1993 for the General Synod of the Church of England
by Church House Publishing

General Synod Report of Proceedings November 1992 © The Central Board of Finance
of the Church of England 1993

Supplementary material © The Central Board of Finance of the Church of England 1993

Cover photograph courtesy of the BBC.

Printed in England by Rapier Press Ltd.

CONTENTS

FOREWORD

November 11th, 1992 was by any standards an historic day in the life of the Church of England. For some, the General Synod's decision, by majorities of over two-thirds in each of Synod's three Houses, to give final approval to the draft legislation on the ordination of women to the priesthood was a major step forward in the recognition of the ministry of women in the Church. For others, the decision represented the abandonment of the Church of England's claim to be part of the one, holy, catholic and apostolic Church.

The vote was the culmination of a synodical process which had begun seventeen years earlier when the General Synod passed a motion 'That this Synod considers that there are no fundamental objections to the ordination of women to the priesthood'.

The story of that process is briefly set out in the concluding section of this book. The process did not finish on 11 November. Because of the established status of the Church of England, the legislation has now gone forward to Parliament for consideration. It will be at least another year and probably longer after the vote before, if Parliament approves, the first woman is ordained priest.

The Synod's debate was notable for many reasons. It began and ended in prayer, and many afterwards commented not only on the quality of the contributions but on the sensitive and charitable atmosphere in which, in spite of strong emotions clearly expressed, it was conducted. Through radio and television many who were not regular churchgoers were able to follow the debate and found themselves caught up in it.

Since the debate, there have been several requests that the record of it should be published. This book is a response to those requests. You will find in it an exact and complete account of what was said, together with brief biographical notes about each speaker and background information which sets the proceedings in context. It is both an accurate record of an historic day and a contribution to the continuing debate throughout the universal Church on the ordination of women to the priesthood.

Philip Mawer

Church House, SW1   *Secretary General*
December 1992   *of the General Synod*

WEDNESDAY 11 NOVEMBER 1992

The Archbishop of York (Dr John Habgood) *took the Chair at 10.00 a.m.*
Prayers were said by The Chairman.

LEGISLATIVE BUSINESS

Draft Priests (Ordination of Women) Measure (GS 830C)

Draft Canon C 4B (Of Women Priests) (GS 831C)

Draft Amending Canon No 13 (GS 832C)

Draft Ordination of Women (Financial Provisions) Measure (GS 833C)

LEGISLATION FOR FINAL APPROVAL

The Chairman: I declare on behalf of the Presidents, the Prolocutors and the Chairman and Vice-Chairman of the House of Laity that the requirements of Article 7 and Article 8 have been complied with in respect of these items of business.

Members will already have seen the special arrangements for this debate set out in the paper SecGen(92)15, and will realise that the aim is to have one principal debate on Item 502 in which we hope the whole range of concerns will be covered, so that if this is passed we can then move on quickly through the remaining motions. There is a hope that we may be ready to vote on Item 502 somewhere round 4.30, but this of course depends on the Synod because, in a final approval debate, the number of procedural motions that you can have is severely limited. (If you want to find out what they are, look at Standing Order 72.) In particular, it is not permitted in this kind of debate to move the closure. This creates problems when, as now, there are more than 200 requests to speak.

I should mention that one of those requests to speak came from Carol Watson who would certainly have been called had she lived and who desperately wanted to speak in this debate.

It means that some self-discipline will be necessary on everybody's part, and the Chair must rely on the good sense of speakers to be brief, not to repeat things which have already been said and, as we proceed in the afternoon, to be sensitive to the mood of the Synod as to when we have all had enough. The only weapon that the Chair has is in imposing speech limits, which will be adhered to very rigidly, no matter who is speaking.

The arrangement is that we shall have two opening speakers, both of whom will be given 15 minutes. The second of them will, exceptionally, be allowed to speak again at the end of the debate in the winding-up process. There are also two designated speakers who will be given slightly longer than others to restart the debate after lunch. After the two opening speakers a 10-minute speech limit will be in operation.

The Bishop of Guildford (Rt Revd Michael Adie):   I beg to move:

'That the Measure entitled "Priests (Ordination of Women) Measure" be finally approved.'

When the Speaker of the House of Commons, Betty Boothroyd, presented herself to the Lords Commissioners for confirmation of her appointment, she requested for the Commons, in accordance with ancient custom, that 'the most favourable construction shall be put upon all their proceedings'. The Lord Chancellor assured Madam Speaker that 'Her Majesty will ever place the most favourable construction upon your words and actions'. In this debate and in the actions that flow from it we all ask that the best construction be put upon our words and, conversely, we avoid attributing base or unworthy motives to others. We are here today not aggressively to drive our convictions through and to defeat opponents but as representatives of the Church together searching for the truth for us today. Truth is not something that we impose on others; it is revealed to us, it is to be recognised, and it is to be acted on.

Many of us find that those whose judgment we respect and whose friendship we value hold views on the ordination of women to the priesthood different from our own. We are all sensitive that the decision made today, whatever it is, will cause pain to some whom we have no desire to hurt. Nonetheless a decision must be made and we must listen and reason in order that the wisest way forward may be found. In August this year the Anglican province of South Africa debated this issue. It is reported that Archbishop Desmond Tutu pleaded that people should see that, though we disagree and disagree vehemently, yet we remain friends. One who disagreed with their final decision said that he was gravely disappointed by the vote; 'I am moved, however, by the spirit of synod, which throughout the debate was loving and prayerful'. We trust that the same will be said at the end of our debate today.

This determination to stay together has shaped the legislation now before us. Many on both sides of the debate would have preferred a one-clause Measure plainly and simply providing for women to be ordained to the priesthood. The report of 1986, prepared by a group representing all points of view, recognised that a one-clause Measure would not do. The House of Bishops in its 1987 report agreed, and the Synod endorsed the Bishops' report, so setting the shape of the legislation. There must be provisions which ensure that those who do not agree with the ordination of women still have room and space in the Church of England. Hence the provisions for bishops, clergy and parishes. These ensure that people with different views and different theologies will still have a respected and secure place in the Church. During the course of our debates those provisions have been adjusted by the Synod in response to criticism, and they are now as good as corporately we can make them. Furthermore, they are secure because they cannot be withdrawn or altered except by another Measure.

Legislation can take us only so far along the road towards space and openness, so the code of practice indicates the sensitivity with which the legislation will be implemented. I want to add to that, as a steady Church of England man (to use Dr Johnson's phrase) that I, fellow bishops and many others will work strenuously to keep space and room in every ministry of the Church for those who for different reasons have difficulty with the ordination of women. The strength of the Church of England ever since the Reformation has been its ability to hold together Catholic and Reformed — not in uneasy juxtaposition but in interaction. Of course that can be lampooned and trivialised as woolliness and compromise, but our strength as a Church is that, while being loyal to our tradition and our formularies, yet we retain within the Church people and theologies which stimulate and complement one another. As has been said, 'The opposite of a correct statement is a false statement, but the opposite of a profound truth may well be another profound truth.' Those of us who believe that it is right to take the decision to ordain women to the priesthood are determined to keep space for those of a different view. Not only is the legislation generous in its provisions, but the Church must retain its traditional generosity of spirit.

In recent times the Church of England has been enriched by women authorised as Readers, deaconesses and deacons. Those of us on both sides of the debate who have observed and experienced that ministry want to say to those women that they have enlarged our minds and won our respect for what they have done and are doing in a Church which does not make life easy for them. The question now to be decided, however, is whether women, as well as being Readers and deacons, should also be priests. I put to the Synod that the answer is yes; the ordination of women to the priesthood is a reasoned development consonant with Scripture and required by tradition.

The profound truth of the Bible with regard to men and women is that both men and women are made in the image of God. That is the fundamental truth of Genesis, picked up by Jesus (according to the gospels) and alluded to by St Paul in his letter to the Galatians: man and woman are complementary to one another, equal but distinct partners, and together they make up humanity fit for friendship with God. That fundamental scriptural truth remains whichever way our vote goes today. If woman has been regarded or treated as subservient to man, that is because of our human failure, that twisting of God's purpose which we call the Fall. St Paul may well be unclear on the place of women in the Church but that is because he is wrestling with making sense of our failure to grasp the divine truth of man and woman together being in the image of God. The Scriptures are inconclusive on the question of the ordination of women; they are firm and conclusive on man and woman together being in the image of God.

Our traditional and basic understanding of the Incarnation is that in Jesus Christ God took human nature and became embodied as a human person. He took human nature. Human nature or humanity is available in only two forms, male and female, and God when incarnate had to be one or the other. That does not mean that, whichever he had chosen, we would for all time have a one-gender ministry of the same sex as he chose. God became incarnate as a man rather than a woman, but in becoming man he took human nature which comprises both male and female. For centuries we have accepted men in the priesthood as the automatic consequence of God taking human nature, but then for centuries it was only men who enjoyed education, political leadership, the vote and so on, and these have only gradually, even grudgingly, become available to women. What God has made clear to us in our century is that women are not inferior to men, nor are they identical; men and women are complementary; together and equally they make up humanity. That simple but fundamental truth which God has shown to us in his world now resonates with a renewed understanding of the Scriptures.

Once that simple truth has enlightened our minds we have to look again at our tradition. The ordained ministry is representative of the whole people of God, male and female. It is also representative of Christ who is the God who assumed human nature. Now that we see clearly that male and female together in complementarity constitute human nature, to exclude either male or female from ordained ministry is to risk being lop-sided in our understanding and expression of truth.

Furthermore, we now not only need women in the priesthood to offer their distinctive ministry alongside that of men, we need men and women and the interaction between them. As the writer of Ecclesiasticus put it, 'All things go in pairs, by opposites, and he has made nothing defective: the one consolidates the excellence of the other'.

To argue for women in the priesthood is not to say now that previous ministry has been defective; it is, rather, that an old truth now seen in a new context requires us to express tradition differently if we are to preserve in our time the truth as we have inherited it. The ordination of women to the priesthood may be contrary to tradition in the sense that it has not happened before; it is not contrary to tradition in the sense of truth as it has been handed down to us. Indeed, if we are to be faithful to tradition in the light of contemporary truth, this development is required of us.

When developments take place in the life of the Church they usually happen piecemeal, as groups of Christians perceive a truth and give it expression; it is rare for the Church to sit back and make a decision to move ahead uniformly. The Reformation or the Oxford Movement did not happen evenly as a result of corporate decision; they struggled forward place by place, country by country. That is the untidy way in which developments happen. Many of us wish that the decision to ordain women to the priesthood could be taken by the Churches of Rome and the East with the Anglicans in formal agreement, but that is not a realistic hope at the present time – and we must bear in mind that in formal terms, whatever the local reality, the Roman Catholic communion does not accept the validity of any Anglican orders. Although we must always listen to and learn from other Churches, both those who ordain women and those who do not, the reality is that we must make up our minds, accept responsibility for our decisions and make our contribution to the diverse life of the Church. As this development takes place it will happen untidily, with various provinces and Churches making their own decisions.

So I put to the Synod that the ordination of women to the priesthood is a reasoned development, consonant with Scripture, required by tradition. Whatever the outcome of our debate today there will be continuing discussion on the relationship between men and women and on the nature of ministry; these are profound issues and our debate and decision today cannot settle such matters once and for all. Whatever decision we make today, we are all engaged in a process and we have continuing work to do together. We have, however, reached a point of decision. We have discussed the issue of women in the priesthood for many years; we have gained experience of women as deacons; the theological argument has moved steadily in favour; we have consulted across the Church and there is a clear majority judging this step to be right. So now let us move forward with conviction, confident in God who leads us into truth. This is a step whose time has come.

The Archdeacon of Leicester (Ven. David Silk): Among the great cloud of witnesses which surrounds us as a Synod today is Thomas More, Chancellor of England and martyr. In his Confutation of Tyndale's Answer, More comments on religious controversy in these moving and prayerful words: 'Sometime [God] showeth [his truth] leisurely, suffering his flock to commune and dispute thereupon. And in their treating of the matter suffereth them with good mind and scripture . . . to search and seek for the truth, and to vary for a little while in their opinions, till that he reward their virtuous diligence with leading them secretly into the consent and concord and belief of the truth by his Holy Spirit.'

Consent, concord, truth, Holy Spirit. We have consulted the dioceses and the deaneries, and the result is by no means conclusive. Had a two-thirds majority in each House been required, as we require today, only 41 per cent of the deanery synods and only 52 per cent of the diocesan synods would have carried the legislation. Moreover, although the vote was on the actual legislation the members of synods often encountered misunderstanding. Sadly, they heard, 'We must discuss the principle; the legislation can be amended.' Of course it cannot. In any case, it is as representatives and not as delegates that we stand at the final hurdle and must make up our minds. *(The fire alarm bell rang.)*

The Chairman: Unfortunately, the hall must be evacuated because there is a suspect bomb or fire alert in the building. I therefore adjourn the Synod under Standing Order 14 until such time as we are informed that business may resume. Will all members please leave the hall by the nearest emergency route and leave the building without delay?

(Short adjournment)

The Chairman: Perhaps the fact that it was a false alarm is a good omen! I will give the Archdeacon of Leicester a little extra time, 15 minutes from the end of his quotation from Sir Thomas More.

The Archdeacon of Leicester: Thank you, Your Grace. As I was saying ... !

Consent, concord, truth, Holy Spirit. We have consulted the dioceses and deaneries, and the result is by no means conclusive. Had a two-thirds majority in each House been required, as we require here today, only 41 per cent of the deanery synods and only 52 per cent of the diocesan synods would have carried the legislation. Moreover, although the vote was on the actual legislation, the members of synods often encountered misunderstanding. They heard, 'We must discuss the principle; the legislation can be amended.' In any case, it is as representatives and not delegates that we stand now at the final hurdle and must make up our minds.

We must be clear. This debate is not about the undisputed value of the pastoral and preaching ministry of women, it is about this legislation. It is not about a career structure, since the ordained ministry is only by accident a career but by nature an order, irrespective of preferment and remuneration, it is about this legislation. It is not about deeply rooted sexism in the Church, about discrimination against women, although there are continuing problems in that area which I do not take lightly; the debate is about this legislation. We are asked not merely for general approval of the ordination of women to the priesthood but for specific approval that it be done, here and now, by this means and at whatever cost. The rightness or wrongness of the general principle bears upon our decision, but the decision is yes or no to the detailed provisions of GS 830C.

The legislation, then. 'Legal measures,' declares Yves Congar, 'imply a particular theology.' What sort of theology is shown forth by this legislation? For a start, a provisional ministry. Can there be anything provisional about a ministry on which depend the sacraments of the Church? The catechism describes the sacraments as 'an outward and visible sign of an inward and spiritual grace given unto us, ordained by Christ himself, as a means whereby we receive the same, and a pledge to assure us thereof'. There is nothing provisional about pledges and assurances, and in my living and at my dying I do not want to hear anything provisional, thank you. The notion of reception is a related idea and sadly misleading. In all conscience, a ministry that the bishops describe as 'intimately related to the centre of the faith' cannot be received as a form of service or a conciliar statement.

Clause 1(1) of the Measure solves at a stroke two knotty theological issues with breath-taking self-assurance: 'It shall be lawful for the General Synod to make provision by Canon for enabling a woman to be ordained to the office of priest'. Those then who have deep reservations about these proposals on the scriptural grounds of headship, and those who have deep reservations grounded in revelation and expressed in what may be called, for convenience, the 'representative' arguments, are flatly and boldly told that their reservations are without foundation. The invariable practice of two thousand years is terminated in a single sub-clause. Has then the Church been totally mistaken for two thousand years, hoodwinked, infected by social and cultural conditioning? If that is what is contended, it must be fully and properly spelled out in this debate today. The burden of proof is fairly and squarely on the proponents of the Measure. Supporters of the 'headship' and of the 'representative' arguments must be convinced beyond all reasonable doubt. If not convinced, they must vote no.

I refer to the 'headship' issue and the 'representative' issue together because they have certain significant things in common. For example, both groups agree firmly that when St Paul writes in Galatians 'In Christ there is neither male nor female' he is speaking about baptism rather than ordination and our oneness in Christ does not affect our identity and purpose in creation. Both affirm that the Church's knowledge of God's holy will and saving grace depends on revealed truth rather than human wisdom. Thus the advocates of change must explain their view in relation to our Article VI, which insists that 'Holy Scripture containeth all things necessary to salvation: so that whatsoever is not read therein, nor may be proved thereby, is not to be ... thought requisite or necessary to salvation.' The plain truth is that the ordination of women to the presbyterate is not prescribed by Holy Scripture nor may it be proved thereby. It is a new orthodoxy.

Clause 1(1) of the Measure introduces yet another novelty for which there is no warrant in Scripture, provincial autonomy. We must then consider the authority of the Church, the authority that Jesus received from the Father and handed on. This authority, the pledge of Christ's presence and the basis of our unity, is exercised at appropriate levels by Christ in his Church. There are decisions affecting the life of the Church which can properly be taken at parish or deanery or diocesan or provincial level; and there are decisions which can only be taken, if at all, by the universal Church. There are certain things – the canon of Scripture, the text of the creeds, the matter of the sacraments – in which the local Church has no authority to legislate. The Church of England's formularies, Canon A 1 and the Declaration of Assent assert that the Church of England is 'part of the one, holy, catholic and apostolic Church', and so subject to its authority.

The Scriptures know of two manifestations of the Church: the universal Church and the local Church gathered round its bishop. This legislation invites a provincial synod, without warrant in either Scripture or tradition, to act as though it were an ecumenical council. One hears it said, 'They are our orders, we can do what we like with them.' You might as well say, 'It's our faith, we can do what we like with it'!

Now to clause 1(2) which at a stroke solves another theological riddle: 'Nothing in this Measure shall make it lawful for a woman to be consecrated to the office of bishop.' While the New Testament does not give us a clear blueprint for the ordained ministry, it is at least evident beyond dispute that in the New Testament there is no distinction between presbyter and bishop. While later developments have reserved to the bishop certain responsibilities, the two are essentially one order. It is intended of course that the Church should become accustomed to women priests before considering the possibility of women bishops, but this clause discriminates against women, confuses the theology of order by driving a wedge between the episcopate and the presbyterate, and invites the Synod to vote for legislation barring women from the episcopate, knowing full well that more far-reaching legislation may soon enough appear. Is it not procedure by stealth rather than by principle?

In clause 2 we have more theological confusion and pastoral mayhem. Nonsense is made of the office of bishop as Lambeth 1988 described him, 'the family's centre of life and love'. The Measure provides that bishops appointed after the relevant date may not make the declaration excluding women priests. To be sure, the code of practice, which is said in its preface to be 'not part of the legislation, and it will be open to the House of Bishops to alter or add to it,' does provide in section 39 (iv) for bishops who do not wish to ordain women to allow others to ordain in their dioceses. In other words, a bishop may become a bishop provided that he is not going to act like one, provided that he is willing to let someone else do that which he does not believe ought to be done, in order to ordain as priests people whose priesthood he, the diocesan bishop and father-in-God, will not recognise and with whom he may not be in communion. It is fairyland. The House of Bishops said in 1987 that such an arrangement would 'destroy the relationship of a bishop to his diocese'. Whatever line a bishop takes under this clause, his ministry will be unacceptable to some of his flock. Similarly, although the legislation permits a bishop in office to exclude the ministry of women priests in his diocese, incumbents remain free to invite them to their parishes for limited periods. What price the bishop as focus of unity?

The Measure enshrines in the law a disputed and disunited ministry. Clause 3 places the authority to recognise the authenticity of a minister at the parish level. What holds the Church of England together — and the Bishop of Guildford referred to this — is our characteristic relationship between uniformity of practice and pluralism of belief. Creeds and liturgical texts hold together a variety of theological perspectives. A number of varying opinions about the significance of bishops in the divine economy are held together by the invariable practice of episcopal ordination, and all our clergy are recognised without dispute. If this legislation is carried, some ministers will, with the sanction of the law, not be recognised by some of their colleagues or by some of our parishes.

Yet the bishops said in GS 764, 'What is barely tolerable between provinces would be even more acutely felt between and within dioceses of a single province.' 'I am of Cephas and I am of Apollos' will be a reality in the diocese, in the deanery, in the parish, in hearth and home. How far can the legislation apply its alleged wisdom and charity to the areas where there is no choice of church or minister? Division will go right to the altar rail itself.

The legislation simply phases out the objectors. You may bandy about the words 'provisional' and 'reception' and 'co-existence' as much as you wish, but built into the essential fabric of the legislation is a sustained bias towards a predetermined acceptance of women priests. If there can be no more diocesan bishops opposed, unless they are prepared to be mere druids dispensing sacraments without a full pastoral relationship, opponents will be increasingly and designedly deprived of episcopal care and leadership and of other participation in the life of the Church, and will be left to wither and die.

Those who advocate this legislation must answer six objections to it. First, it proposes irreversible action arising from a theology which cannot be demonstrated beyond all reasonable doubt to be required by Scripture as understood by the Church through the ages. Second, it proposes that action in a primary matter of faith and order by an authority which is claimed without the precedent of Scripture or the tradition of the Church. Third, it makes a false separation between the episcopate and the presbyterate and in so doing discriminates against women. Fourth, it makes theological and pastoral non-sense of the office of the bishop as focus of unity and replaces episcopacy with a confection of mere congregationalism and sheer papalism. Fifth, it lacks a sufficient consensus in the Church at every level and enshrines the division firmly in a law which requires another two-thirds majority in order to change it. Sixth, it is wholly biased in the direction of the inexorable phasing-out of objection. There can be no co-existence for there are no equal terms.

The legislation is described as wise and charitable. I fear I see in it the sly wisdom of a Solomon proposing to carve up the baby and the cold charity of a Dives towards Lazarus at the gate. In the spirit of Thomas More with whose wise words I began, I urge the Synod to agree that a consensus has not been achieved, that this legislation is neither wise nor charitable and that this is neither the right time nor the right way to proceed.

Dr Christina Baxter (Southwell): When people talk about the theology of ordination in our Church of England, it soon becomes clear that they take one of two options as the main reference point in their thinking: either they define ordination in relationship to the sacraments and particularly the Eucharist, or they define ordination in relationship to the Word of God which is taught and applied to the Church in government. Roughly speaking, these are the Catholic and Reformed positions, and it is to the second of them that I wish to speak today as I support this legislation.

If ordination is to the ministry of the Word, preached and taught and applied in discipline and encouragement, what light does the New Testament shed on the question of whether we should vote for this legislation? At supper last night, one of my synodical colleagues said that nothing new could be said today and we had better keep silence and then vote. While I have a great deal of sympathy with that view, it is not true for me that nothing new has emerged between July and November. During the past four months I have reviewed all the arguments from my Evangelical roots and I have stood on the edge of an abyss, since many recent opponents from that tradition have argued in such a way that not only my convictions about women's ordination but also my convictions about the place of laywomen have been called into question. It is a very solemn thing to wonder whether the past 20 years of preaching, teaching and offering spiritual counsel have been not only ill advised but plain contrary to God's will, and that is what I had to ask myself as a layperson involved in those ministries.

Synod may be helped to know that although I signed a blank cheque to God about twenty years ago to go into any kind of ministry, I have never been called to be ordained, so my advocacy of this legislation today is only so that I may receive the ministry of my sisters as I have in other parts of the world.

While I have been living in the turmoil of allowing myself to entertain all these questions again, I have also had cause to ponder deeply on the whole of chapter 9 of John where the man who is born blind is healed by Jesus and then abandoned to a terrible inquisition, from his friends, neighbours, Pharisees, leaders of the religious parties of the time and parents, about whether and how his healing happened, who did it, whether this Jesus was from God or a sinner who broke the sabbath law. In the midst of this immense pressure of questioning, the man who has been healed from blindness models the tension between confident retelling of what his testimony knows and frank admission of what

16

he certainly does not know and simply cannot understand. Just when relief seems at hand, because all have abandoned him and Jesus re-finds him, we are startled to hear Jesus continue the inquisition with some questions as searching as those we face in the baptism service of today, a kind of 'Do you turn to Christ?'

It is that context in which I understand myself and my synodical colleagues to stand today. There are some things of which we are certain, others where we frankly do not know, but we must recognise that when Jesus returns to us at the end time, as he returned to the man who had been healed, it will not be to answer our questions about this package of legislation but to ask us yet more searching questions about our commitment and our discipleship. So although I would love to ask Synod to vote unanimously for this legislation today, I cannot ask anyone to do anything which would preclude them from standing in the circle of God's love as Jesus comes to put to them, as he will come to put to me, the same gracious, searching questions at the last.

So what has led me as a Reformed Evangelical Anglican to decide that this is the right step to take now? My first reason is that I do not think that Scripture forbids it. The New Testament, contrary to many who write about it, knows nothing about headship, though some of the letters refer to man as head of woman. Until 1985 it was commonly assumed that *kephale* or head could mean 'source', as in the head or source of a river, or 'ruler', as in the head of a house. This has been called into question by Wayne Grudem, an American scholar with a Cambridge PhD, in an article which examines over 2,300 uses of *kephale* in literature of the same period as the New Testament. He argues that 'source' is nowhere the meaning of head and 'ruler' is often its meaning. A flurry of articles followed, and Grudem answered his detractors towards the end of 1990. Time does not allow me to go into details, but it is an interesting debate. I did not know that when the Hebrew Old Testament was translated into Greek the Hebrew word for head, *rosh*, when it means 'ruler', is very rarely translated by *kephale* as 'head': eight times only in 109. So clearly while *kephale* rarely means 'source' it equally rarely means 'ruler'.

Only two conclusions may be drawn from this. First, neither side can be as certain as it thought it could be about what 'head' means in the New Testament; second, we need to resort to a good interpretive principle and let the context decide. When someone shouts 'fire' we have to look to see what the circumstances are (*laughter*), whether to fall flat on the pavement to avoid the bullets or throw on a bucket of water. So let us briefly look at the context of one example in the New Testament. In Ephesians 5 the husband is spoken of as the head of the wife, and many would argue that the marriage pattern is part of the creation pattern: what is good for Christian households is good for the household of God. What, however, does the context say? That the husband is

17

to love his wife as Christ loves the Church and gave himself up for her. Clearly, *kephale* or 'head' here means to imitate Christ as suffering servant and not Christ as king. Pressed by an Evangelical friend in the summer, I said that I thought it would be easy to submit to such a love in marriage, but I now think I was wrong. Writing for a context in which men had authority and women submitted, Ephesians is saying to husbands, 'Give away status and power as Jesus did', and to wives, 'Submit yourselves to loving service'. I own that this is hard for me and maybe for all women who are more used to serving than being served; I identify very closely with the Peter who grabbed the towel and the bowl, confronted with the kneeling, serving and washing Jesus. That helps me to understand how we can be commanded to be subject to one another out of reverence for Christ but also why women might especially be encouraged to receive this kind of service.

Those of Synod who are deepest into this kind of argument will know that 1 Corinthians 11 is far harder than Ephesians 5, mentioning man as head of his wife. Here I have to admit that I do not know all the ins and outs, although I do know what the possibilities are. I am glad that what is considered by New Testament scholars to be one of the best modern commentaries on 1 Corinthians, that by Gordon Fee, simply says of verse 10, which is the crux of the argument, that it is a text so difficult that it has defied our best scholarly guesses over centuries. I merely add that it is interesting that in that passage, although we do not often hear it, the only person who has authority mentioned is the woman, though it is often translated 'veil'.

Similarly I have recently read a book by some people called Kroeger on the 1 Timothy passage about authority; they suggested a radical revision of the traditional understanding of that passage, to be seen against the sects clearly confronted in the rest of the epistle. Our author is saying that women can be women, they can be wives and mothers, and be saved, and they are to submit not to men but to Scripture, and to learn.

Positively, I think that there are three reasons for going ahead with the legislation, theological, practical and financial. We have rediscovered plural leadership and we have rediscovered in the New Testament flexibility of ministry. There are practical things which point us in that way — the missionary situation of our Church today and the opportunity to plant churches in our own nation. Then there are the financial constraints, the strain put on those who currently exercise ministry and the need for a new pattern of collaborative ministry which I believe women especially are able to offer.

I vote not in fear but in confidence in a God who can choose and use Jacob the cheat, David the murderer and adulterer, Peter the denier. This God can certainly choose and use the Church of England which is not deliberately seeking to sin but, prayerfully, to do what is right.

The Bishop of London (Rt Revd and Rt Hon David Hope): It is with considerable reluctance and real anguish that I offer my contribution to this debate for, whatever happens at the end of today as we come to vote on the legislation before us, we know that the question will not be entirely resolved. It is one which is on the agenda of almost every Church throughout the world at this time and, whichever way the Synod votes, this issue simply will not go away.

I am not, nor ever have been, one of those who believe that it is impossible ever for a woman to be ordained. Furthermore, I have sought wherever possible to affirm, to support and to encourage the ministry of women both in my previous diocese of Wakefield and in my present diocese of London. I am totally committed to the full-time ministry of women in the Church, but I am not yet fully convinced that this should necessarily be in the context of the ministerial priesthood or episcopate. So I must confess that I am one of those who remain uncertain, still grappling seriously, very seriously indeed, with questions unresolved in my heart and mind. I hope that I can say in all honesty that I am very open to the fact that I may well be wrong.

However, today's debate is about a certain legislative package that is before us, a series of proposals to put into effect the ordination of women to the priesthood, and it is here that I am considerably more certain that this legislation has not got it right. In fact, I have strong hesitations and reservations about its aims, its tone and its possible effects on the Church of England. I believe that, as a Synod, we should have the courage to face the fact that we have not got it right.

I speak further as someone who, from the very moment of having been entrusted with episcopal ministry in the Church some seven years ago, has been personally involved in seeking as constructive a way forward as possible, and also as one who has been involved more widely in the Anglican Communion with the work of the Eames Commission, a commission which as much as anything sought to ensure a real and continuing space for those unable to accept the ordination of women to the ministerial priesthood and episcopate. So there are two particular points that I would like to address.

The first is the statement in one of the documents issuing from the Movement for the Ordination of Women that following a vote in favour this legislation 'makes provision for everyone to carry on as usual'. If the twelve (or however many they turn out to be at the end of the day) diocesan bishops opposed to the legislation actually made all the declarations under clause 2, which they would be perfectly entitled to do, and which are included as having been given as 'a generous offer from the majority to the minority', so making it impossible for women to minister in their dioceses, would this be carrying on as usual? Potentially at least, that number of dioceses would be closed on the very grounds of ministerial order, not because of finance or numbers or strategy but simply and solely on the grounds of that order which I believe to be of the very essence of the Church, where the interchangeability of ordained ministers is a potent sign of communion, of what it actually means to be a Church.

If we are really not expecting the provisions of this particular clause to be used, why are they there at all? I believe and have consistently argued that clause 2 should not stand part of this legislation. If the legislation is passed, in spite of the scenario that I have just set out (but which is a real possibility), my view anyway is that life would become quite intolerable and indeed impossible for any bishop who made every one of those declarations. It looks like generosity; I do not believe that it is. Without doubt, however, its use even to a more limited extent would affect the life of the Church of England, as indeed would the provisions for parishes in clause 3.

Again, what of some of the provisions in the draft code of practice? Note that the code of practice is only a draft at this stage, so there must be some question of whether it will remain as it is or whether it may yet be changed beyond all recognition.

My second point, and one which gives me the greatest concern, however, is the position of those who are opposed, for whatever reason, if the legislation goes forward. It is argued that the provisions of Part II are offered generously for the well-being and inclusion of those so opposed. I am not personally convinced. The revision committee's report GS 830Y indicates the clear understanding of those who are promoting this legislation, and Synod should be in no doubt about it. Indeed I would not expect anything other from those who are so firmly convinced that they are right. The report concludes that 'the necessary majority in its favour [today] would indicate that a common mind on the issue had in fact been achieved within the Church of England', a statement that I certainly question and challenge. The revision committee's report further states that when the legislation came into force it would express the mind of the Church of England on the issue of women priests, 'that women priests must be accepted with theological and ecclesiological integrity and that their acceptance must become the new theological understanding of the Church of England'. Also the safeguards, as Part II is described, are intended in order to 'give opponents an opportunity to plan their future'. That does not sound very much like well-being and inclusion to me.

Such a view was further underscored by a member of the same committee presenting the legislation in the debate in 1989 when, it was said, 'We must never lose sight of the basic fact that the various safeguards of [Part II] are unusual and exceptional', as indeed they are, 'exceptional provisions . . . given by the majority to the minority with very strong views'. And why? The reason is very plain indeed: "so that that minority may have space to assess the reality of the ordination of women as it takes place in our provinces. However, because the provisions are exceptional they must in the end be seen as temporary.'

Those who are opposed are now being given considerable reassurances that all will be well, that the Church of England will continue as ever it has and that there is a full and equal place for all, particularly those who are unable to accept the ordination of women as priests. I submit that the reality would be very different indeed, that if this legislation is passed the Church of England will without doubt be very different and that those unable to accept this new theological understanding with theological and ecclesiological integrity will inevitably and increasingly find themselves ignored and marginalised.

Having said this, I shall try to respect, with as good and generous a grace as I can, whatever decision is reached at the end of this day, praying that God will indeed give me the necessary grace and wisdom to continue in communion and fellowship with all in my diocese, whatever their views, and, I desperately hope and pray, they with me too.

The Archbishop of Canterbury (Dr George Carey): I want to begin by thanking the Bishop of London for that thoughtful and sensitive speech, even though I will be disagreeing with him.

The Church of England is no stranger to days of decision like this. At such times we are caught between faith and fear, between the excitement of a new experience and the fear of the risk involved. We are fearful for the Church's unity for we know that God wills his Church to be one. We are fearful too that this decision could irretrievably fracture the tradition and character of the ordained priesthood as we have inherited it. I believe, however, that these fears, which in various ways we all share, are not well grounded. God calls us to take the risk of faith. I believe that God is also calling his Church to ordain women to the priesthood.

As the Bishop of Guildford has reminded us, we come to this debate well prepared. This is no precipitate measure foisted on an unwilling Church; it has been on the Synod's agenda for nearly twenty years. We have experienced the ministry of well over a thousand women in the diaconate. Elsewhere in the Anglican communion women priests are exercising increasingly important ministries. At diocesan and deanery levels the voting on this legislation clearly demonstrates that it is looked on with favour by the majority of our people. We have made haste slowly. That is because we want as broad a measure of unity as we can manage. Today we look for a two-thirds majority of all those voting in each House; few secular governing bodies set such a demanding threshold, but this is a sign of our care for unity.

Despite all this, some members may still wonder whether this is an unprecedented risk for the Church to take. Like Dr Baxter I want to go back to Scripture. Let us look for guidance to one of the key moments of decision in the Church's life. In Acts 10 God challenges Peter's assumption that the Gospel is only for the Jews. Members will recall the stages. First it begins with what is familiar. Peter repeatedly dreams about the food laws; he thinks he knows all about them. God challenges us to begin in the world that we know. Today we are looking at a familiar world of priests and vicars, Church and society, gifts and leadership. We are being challenged to do something new, but it is in the context of what we already know so well, just as it was for Peter.

Second, messengers take Peter to Cornelius the centurion. Peter finds, to his astonishment, that the Spirit has already been given to the Gentiles. God has been working outside the traditions and categories with which Peter is familiar. We too are being challenged to reconsider what God has been doing outside our familiar world in the light of our changed situation.

The final stage is reached as Peter interprets his vision in the light of his new experience. He sees that God does call the Gentiles into the Body of Christ. God has shown that what seems novel and risky is consonant with what has happened in the past. I believe that the same dynamic is at work today. I want to remind Synod that the inclusion of the Gentiles within the Body of Christ was not as obvious at the time as it now appears. It seemed to be a major break with tradition. Today we are considering what some believe to be another break with tradition. That is not the case. We are not departing from a traditional concept of ministry, we are talking about an extension of the same ministry to include women. Christianity is all about God liberating, renewing and drawing out what has been there implicitly from the beginning.

Some will argue that we have no right to make such changes on our own, and we know that the Roman Catholic Church and the Orthodox Churches do not at present countenance this change. That, however, cannot be an obstacle to the Church of England determining its own mind. Article XX makes it clear that the Church of England 'hath . . . authority in Controversies of Faith'. I am well aware that there are those who are profoundly troubled by the ecumenical implications of a yes vote today. I recognise that, but this consideration is not completely overriding. I believe that constructive and loving relationships with our sister Churches can and will continue, whatever the outcome of the vote today. Significant parts of Christendom do not ordain women to the priesthood but there are many traditions in which the experience of women in ministry is not a burden but a joy, not a handicap to mission but a strength. We must not look in one direction only.

Beyond all this there lies a wider issue: how do we find God's will in such a matter? My predecessor, Robert Runcie, who patiently guided us through the years of the most heated debate on this subject, comments in his book *Authority in Crisis?* that the Anglican way is essentially that of the *consensus fidelium*. That is to say, it is the gathering together of a response from as many quarters of the Church as possible. Part of that must be in the voting of our diocesan synods which indicates that for our Church most people believe that God's moment, God's *kairos*, has come for us on this issue.

Discernment, however, will not come through votes only but through the manifestation of gifts. Gifts are God's generosity to his people. We have seen the marks of the Spirit increasingly manifest in the ministry of women as well as that of men. We must draw on all available talents if we are to be a credible Church engaged in mission and ministry to an increasingly confused and lost world. We are in danger of not being heard if women are exercising leadership in every area of our society's life save the ordained priesthood.

I am well aware that whatever decision we make will bring pain. Indeed the Anglican way of deciding such matters inevitably involves pain and conflict because the question of truth matters so much to us that as a Church we do not hide our disagreements, we air them in public and we try to find our way through them in a spirit of love and respect for the views of others. That is why our legislation today does not present us with a single-clause Measure; it takes account of those who, in conscience, will have to dissent from it and yet do not wish to leave the Church of England. The associated financial Measure makes provision for those few —and I pray that they may be very few —who feel duty bound to leave the ordained ministry, should we approve the legislation today.

I urge those who see the future only in terms of schism to recognise that disputes about the nature of ministry are not regarded in the New Testament as grounds for formal separation from one's fellow Christians. The step that I hope we shall take today is a development in the Church's tradition. The ordination of women to the priesthood alters not a word in the creeds or the Scriptures or the faith of our Church.

May I add a final reflection about the future? Ours is a Church called to look outwards in mission, to be confident in service and to be prophetic in preaching and teaching. We are also called to be a comprehensive Church in which those who believe on grounds of conscience that women should not be ordained still have an honourable place among us as bishops, clergy and people. I want to repeat that. If the Measure is passed today, I desire that those who still oppose the ordination of women on grounds of conscience should continue to play their full part in the life of our Church. This debate is not about excluding anybody but about enlarging the sympathies and generosity of our Church in line with the generosity of God himself. I hope with all my heart that Synod today will affirm the place of women in the priesthood of Christ's Church as confidently as Peter affirmed the place of the Gentiles long ago. Let us say with him today, 'God gave them no less a gift than he gave us when we put our trust in the Lord Jesus. How could I possibly stand in God's way?'

Mrs Dorothy Chatterley (Carlisle): What is before us this morning for decision is legislation, and from what has been said, and not said, it would appear to be legislation which has attracted few real friends. Perhaps that is not wholly surprising. Clause 1, after all, successfully jettisons revealed truth and ecclesial authority in favour of a unilateral expression of a so-called provincial autonomy quite unknown to the New Testament and expressed in bogus understandings of reception and co-existence which are grounded in a breach of communion and a provisionality of both ministry and sacrament. Clause 2 establishes a novel, two-tier episcopate, successfully ensures that every diocesan bishop is out of communion with at least some of his clergy and makes it impossible, whatever codes of practice may say, for anyone conscientiously opposed to the priestly ordination of women to accept appointment as a diocesan bishop. So to the mistrust of clause 1 is added the marginalisation of clause 2. Clauses 3 and 4 complete the institutionalisation of division with consequent pastoral mayhem at every level of the Church's worshipping and synodical life. Mistrust, marginalisation and mayhem.

This is the legislation, the scenario, that we are invited to approve this morning. Why? Because, some say, the ordination of women is inevitable, so let us get on with it now. I have rarely heard such an unworthy argument ever. We sit here as the chosen representatives of this Church of England, and we are here to judge issues on their merits as they come to us. It is quite immoral to suggest that because some members are persuaded of the rightness of a particular principle the whole of the rest of us should feel obliged to depart from two thousand years of Church teaching and received tradition to accept the very first attempt at a legislative enactment of the principle which is before us.

Then there are some who say 'But we must accept this legislation, flawed though it may be, because our credibility in the world and to the world depends on it.' I had understood from Scripture that we should not seek to be conformed to this world. Indeed, what concerns me is our credibility and integrity as a Church, our manifest loyalty to our title deeds and to our historic faith and ministry which are not to be irreversibly changed —and such change would be irreversible — at the dictates of the world.

Then there is a third group, those who say that we must accept this legislation, warts and all, because it is unfair to those who have a vocation to the priesthood that they should not be tested. I do not for one minute doubt the sincerity of anyone's sense of vocation, but vocation of itself is not sufficient ground for admission to Holy Orders. God has never promised to give us individually all that we feel we should have. Florence Nightingale wrote in her diary, 'I must remind myself that God is not my private secretary.' At times it would seem that an inner call has been quite irrelevant. There was not much evidence of it, was there, in the Apostles' choice of Matthias by lot nor of the episcopal choice of St Ambrose by public acclamation? A sense of personal call requires the irrevocable gift of self. Priesthood is not a career, it is a call to self-abandonment, a total outpouring of self. The Church in her ordinals rightly seeks to discern if there is a sense of call, but then the Church as the living mind of Christ must herself decide whether to ordain either individuals or categories. Certainly there are no automatic rights to testing for either men or women, so claims of pain and hurt in respect of imagined rights are of doubtful validity.

It may well be, as was said in a paper recently sent to Synod members by two Evangelical scholars, that 'it is possible to have greater freedom and fulfilment by living within God's ordained boundaries than by seeking to overthrow them'. In the matter of admission to Holy Orders in the Church of God, and not just the Church of England, we are in the realm of God's grace, of his revealed religion, and of his design for what is his Church. It is from that aspect that we should judge this legislation, and we judge it itself, not from pastoral glosses upon it but by what it actually provides in its terms, its timing, its intended and likely effect, the level of support that it appears to command and the extent to which it fosters and builds up the unity, mission, stability and peace of the One Church, the Body of Christ. In that Church of God we all have a job to do, and it is not the same job, any more than the Persons of the Holy Trinity exercise the same function. Yes, we enjoy an equality, and it is an equality that derives neither from identity of function nor from personal feelings and desires nor from the directives of an Equal Opportunities Commission or the EEC but from God's love for all his creation.

It is because I find in this legislation so little reflection of that comprehension in love, once such a hallmark of the Church of England's polity, that I am persuaded that, whatever one's view on the principle, this dire legislation cannot be supported. St Theresa of Lisieux assures us that we all have but one vocation, and that is to love him who made us and saved us and redeemed us. I hope very much that we shall reject this motion.

Revd June Osborne (London): I stand before Synod today as one who in her own best judgment believes that she might be called to be a priest, and on behalf of many who ask you to keep faith with that sense of calling.

I can describe that conviction as like a developing photograph. When I first began in professional ministry 17 years ago, the image was hazy. What did I then know of priesthood, of myself or of the grace of God? During those 17 years I have learned something of all three. I have been on the staff of four churches and chaplain of a hospital. I have been made a deaconess and ordained a deacon. I have had charge of two parishes, managed a staff team, trained curates and ordinands, led ordination retreats and taught in theological colleges and courses. I think I have learned what is necessary for people who want to know that God is on their side, both inside and outside the Church. So that photograph of myself in priestly ministry has slowly developed, and I have tested it in the ways that have been open to me.

I have tested it in my heart of hearts. I have searched the Scriptures. I have heard what they say about the calling to discipleship and leadership, the call to spiritual and moral integrity, the exercising of gifts, the giving a community of believers vision and nourishing them in the love of Christ. I have tested it by trying to walk faithfully in the tradition of our Church and its beliefs and doctrines, building up the fellowship of the Christian community in pastoral care and preaching, in sacrament and prayer. The Scriptures and the traditions are precious to me – they are my guiding stars in the constellation which is Christ – but they are not enough to test my vocation; the Church itself in its life and in its law must validate that call. Mrs Chatterley is right; that is what we are here to do today. We attend to this legislation so that we may open the way to test the vocation of women like me.

This day, however, is not just about the calling of individual women, it is about the nature and health of our Church, and we are all exercised about what this change will mean for us. Can our Church, in fact, make this change? I think to myself of how the Church is part of redemptive history; the One who has created us is in the process of working our salvation. Communities, Church communities and structures, like individuals, have moments of will when they decide for something new. That may seem radically different at the time, but in many ways we find it consistent with that which has gone before, and the Archbishop of Canterbury has reminded us that so it is with this moment. The road has already been long and we are not unprepared. Quite apart from the intellectual debates of this century we have had five years of women deacons, and the reception of those women deacons ought to give us courage. We have also had an awareness in our time of both the legitimacy of women's voice of faith and its distinctiveness. I think that the vote in deaneries and dioceses, by many who have not yet experienced the ministry of women but have still voted in favour, acknowledges that this moment could be to us health and wholeness.

What of the opposition? What about those who fear that this may be a great and a deep wounding of our Church? Allow me to address the constituency that I know best. Last week a letter went out to some of us under Prebendary John Pearce's address from some who described themselves as Evangelical clergy, calling on us to vote against the motion today. As I looked down these names I realised that a few of them I trained with, many of them are my friends, and all of them are brothers in the Gospel and ministry. So I rang some of them up and for my pains spent many hours in discussion with them. Let me tell Synod what I found.

Many of their concerns were not primarily about the ordination of women. One said he wanted to put up a marker because the Church of England did not take Scripture seriously enough. Another said that the issue for him was lay presidency; if we would allow the presidency of elders, men and women, he would say yes to the ordination of women. Another wanted to protest about what he saw as a move to liberalism. It went on. This legislation was a hook on which some of these men had hung important concerns, but is it fair to make women's vocation a scapegoat?

Some said they wanted to wait for a common mind. Surely, a two-thirds majority, I said, a two-thirds majority in three Houses, is a steep enough hurdle? To raise it higher by asking for total acceptance surely could be interpreted as cynical obstruction? A common mind in matters of community must be by consensus rather than unanimity, and 68.6 per cent in deaneries is, I think, a consensus by another name.

Others were concerned about headship, of which Dr Baxter has spoken. This letter argued that the leadership of women was 'contrary to the plain teaching of Scripture'. I found this a little disingenuous really, for eminent conservative scholars – far more eminent and certainly far more conservative than I – have acknowledged that the relevant texts can be read without either compromising one's care for Scripture or precluding the leadership of women. We may need to disagree on the precise meaning of *kephale*, but I want to sound a warning about this debate: we must beware of basing a whole theology on a single metaphor in the New Testament in isolation from so many others. The arguments around headship shift too quickly, it seems to me, from personal, intimate relationships of marriage to symbolic and structural ones of leadership. The result is that we begin to elevate the significance of gender out of all proportion. Where lies the relevance of my gender when I exercise judgment, teaching, discipline, order, and spiritual endeavour? If we elevate the significance of the gender of the priest we have seen how we very quickly elevate the significance of the gender of Christ, and thus we begin to denigrate women's role in the exercise of faith. We find ourselves straining at gnats and swallowing camels.

Finally, all those to whom I spoke said that this was not an issue for which they would go to the wall, and more than one conceded a secret hope that the legislation would go through either because they found it distracting or because they could actually see that it would bring renewal to us.

To return to my concern for the health of our Church, what will bring salvation to our world and to our shared life? We know salvation if we join ourselves to the creative work of the Spirit, allowing each person and community to fulfil their potential. We know salvation through the victory of forgiving love. Will we allow women, who know so much of suffering love, to carry that into the leadership and particularly into the Eucharist of our Church and thus speak of the Cross in all human experience? We are here today to ask whether we will test vocations. We are asking how we may allow the personality of God to be made transparent by our life together, for a calling to ordination is built on the grace of God – and I long for you to allow me to minister the grace of God through priesthood. In the mercy of Christ and for the sake of our Church, I ask you: please test my vocation.

Revd Peter Geldard (Canterbury): If one looks at the seminal works that describe the foundations of Anglicanism, the book entitled *Anglicanism* by More and Cross or those papers produced for the 1978 and 1988 Lambeth Conferences and edited by Gillian Evans and Robert Wright entitled *The Anglican Tradition* or that modern book which I am sure will become a classic in its time *The Anglican Spirit* by Michael Ramsey, collectively perhaps some two and a half thousand pages of writing, one will not be surprised to discover that the words 'General Synod' do not once appear in those pages. They are works that describe the fundamental claims of Anglicanism, the way that through the Reformation she came into existence, the norms by which she was guided and the principles that she claimed to uphold.

The first thing that she wanted to emphasise was that she was but a part — and a very small part — of a wider Church. At the Reformation, although it was true, to use that common phrase, that she wished to wash her face, she also wanted to emphasise that it was the same face that remained after the reform had taken place. There was renewal, there was reform, yes, but always there was an appeal back to Scripture, to the united Church, to the Ecumenical Councils which she acknowledged and which are enshrined in the Elizabethan Settlement. Above all, through all the vicissitudes of the Reformation, she held on to certain jewels which, in the words of our Prayer Book, are preserved and continued. One of them is the historic ministry which is not ours but a part of something bigger. We are a very small part of the Church that claims to have a common ministry. The orders that people receive are not orders to be priests of the Church of England but priests of the Church of God. In those famous words of Archbishop Fisher, 'We have no Scriptures, Creeds, Sacraments, Apostolic Ministry or Doctrine of our own. We only possess the Scriptures, Creeds, Sacraments, Apostolic Ministry and Doctrine of the Catholic Church which we hold without addition or diminution.'

We are part of a separated part of Christendom, and our glory has been that we have always acknowledged that the price we pay for that is a certain limit and curtailment of what we can do by ourselves. We must be very careful with certain words that we have already used today. How easy it is to slip from 'We, the General Synod' to 'We, the Church of England'; and 'We, the Church of England' quickly becomes 'We, the Anglicans' and then 'The Church has decided'. We are a very small part today, despite the TV cameras and the interest; we are but a provincial synod of two very small parts of Christendom which collectively make up possibly 0.5 per cent of the whole of Christendom. We need to exercise caution in what we claim we can or cannot do.

If we claim that our priesthood, our ordained ministerial priesthood, is not our own but something that we share with others, if we claim to have a common currency with others, we cannot with integrity mint our own coinage and claim that it is the same currency that we are sharing. Yes, we can claim female ministers, we can do something that is *sui generis* to ourselves, but we cannot thereafter ever claim again that we share something with the wider Body of Christ.

We are a very disparate group. As the press look down upon us they must wonder if such a variety of opinions could ever be gathered elsewhere in one room. We surely fulfil the adage that where two or three Anglicans are gathered together there are at least five or six different opinions. Take any subject under the sun and we could easily debate it all day and then divide. Nevertheless, despite our differing opinions this morning we knelt together at the same altar rail and we received the same sacrament, the body and blood of Christ. That happens up and down the land, in the smallest village and in the greatest cathedral, sometimes very simple and sometimes very fancy – and those who know my friends will know that 'very fancy' is indeed an understatement. Yet we kneel together, we share together, we are one together, because we know that, despite the choreography, there is a common understanding of the Word that is spoken, of the bread that is broken and of the person who presides. That gives to our land a unity which breaks through all the divisions and helps us to hold together that comprehensiveness of which we are proud.

Today we are not just asking to push the walls further apart, we are asking to push down one of the walls that holds the very house together, because if this legislation is passed that very act of unity which I have described and which we shared this morning, the very centre and heart of our Church, will become the very sign of our disunity; it will be the place where people cannot be together and from which they must go elsewhere. We will have diocese against diocese, even, within certain towns, parish against parish, and even, in some parishes, parishioners against parishioners. Is that the kind of unity that Christ wishes us to proclaim to the Church at this time? Surely we have got it terribly wrong.

We are not simply dealing today with the ministry of women, not simply with the mere extension, if I may use the Archbishop's words, of the ordained priesthood, we are, I believe, making a radical change which in the past our Church never claimed to have the authority to make. By doing so the Church will pay a major price and, as we have heard, because the legislation is irreversible, it will be an irreparable price.

Let me recount a story which some members know, associated with F.E. Smith (Lord Birkenhead). As I recount it I ask people to remember that today we are talking about the apostolic ministry which has been, we believe, God-given and entrusted to us to share and to hand on and which is not ours to manipulate or to change. There is in the village from which I come a village oak. It has stood there many hundreds of years. It has been a sign and symbol of the strength of the village, to such an extent that it is almost impossible to say whether it is the oak of the village or the village of the oak. Under its boughs brides have been wed and kings have been crowned, peace has been found and pacts have been made. But there comes a new voice in our time, a voice which is very acceptable and sweet. It says that there should be more light and more space. It says there should be more efficiency, and that attempts should be made to change that village oak. Persuasive are their arguments and many seem to go with them. But before one makes that change I ask you to remember this. There are two things they say about the village oak, the greatest of the trees that we have. The first is that, unlike other things that the world possesses, because this is given by God we cannot improve upon it and if we try to change it we can easily destroy the thing itself. Second and more important, they say that that which you see, grand as it is, is but a part and a very small part, for under the ground there are roots and sinews which are bigger and greater than any of us realise, and they go to areas that none of us fully understands.

So I beg of you, Mr Woodman, before you decide to take your axe or even make a change, consider what it is you do, for in your enthusiasm you may change and even destroy more than any of us ever understands.

The Chairman imposed a speech limit of five minutes.

The Bishop of Birmingham (Rt Revd Mark Santer): Members of the Synod will want me, as co-chairman of ARCIC, to say something about the ecumenical implications of the decision that lies before us today, especially from the point of view of the Roman Catholic Church.

There is much more that could be said than there is time for. As I think we all know, there is no doubt that many Roman Catholics believe that women should be ordained to the priesthood. Nevertheless, the official view of the Roman Catholic Church is clear: Christ called only men to the apostolate, and the tradition that men alone may be called to the priesthood has never changed. The Roman Catholic Church does not believe itself to have the authority to vary this tradition.

Roman Catholic colleagues in ARCIC have brought two particular arguments to my attention. First, there is the question of the validity of the sacraments. I quote from a letter that I have received: 'If the Church is in any doubt as to whether it can validly ordain a woman priest to celebrate the Eucharist, it just cannot do it. It must wait until such time as that doubt gives way to a certainty that the Church has such power.' The second argument relates to the nexus of questions round Scripture, tradition and communion. If we are committed to the search for fuller unity (I quote), 'This means, at least, not assuming the authority separately to initiate a radical change in something that touches such a longstanding tradition in the Church.'

The fact that Roman Catholics should be so deeply concerned by our Anglican debate is itself a sign of our growth in love and communion in recent years. If they did not feel a close bond with us, they would not bother to express their concern. This makes it all the more painful to express a contrary view. The fact is that we are concerned for communion with all our fellow Christians, including our fellow Anglicans who do ordain women, and not only for communion with Rome.

This is an issue on which Christians are at present divided, and a choice must be made. It is a very painful position to find ourselves in, but we cannot escape from it. In the long run we must believe that God will show us a way to find one another in one communion in Christ; but in the short run we must make a decision one way or the other.

It is clear that most of the people of the Church of England, not some irresponsible faction but the thoughtful, praying majority of our clergy and laypeople, believe that women as well as men ought to be ordained to the priesthood. I used to believe that it was possible for us to wait for further consensus to develop; I have come to see that continued delay is in fact debilitating the life of the Church.

For me the key issue is the credibility of the Gospel. What kind of Good News is it that only men may represent Christ in the priesthood of the Church? Arguments from authority are indeed indispensable, but in the tradition to which we belong, not only as Anglicans but as Christians of the West, arguments from Scripture and tradition must in the long run commend themselves also to the Christian reason. One cannot argue forever from the letter of Scripture alone or from precedent alone. We have to ask ourselves if it makes sense to the Christian mind.

We must also ask if it makes sense to unbelievers. I have to say this: I cannot see any way in which the liberating power of the Gospel of Christ is commended to an unbelieving world by the assertion that only men may be priests. That for me is the conclusive argument.

The Bishop of Portsmouth (Rt Revd Timothy Bavin): For all of us this debate is surely one of the most difficult and distressing events of our lives, and not one of us here is without hurt, with a pain which has been with us for a long time and which is likely to continue far into the days ahead. For me it arises most of all from the conflict between my heart and my head, for I want women to be ordained to the priesthood and I hope and believe that God may one day lead his Church into that, but I cannot vote for it today. I cannot do so because I do not believe that the Church of England and, in particular, this Synod has reached the point where it can be sure that this is the will of God. We are still deeply divided among ourselves despite years of prayer, debate, experience and reflection.

Moreover we have been subjected to a campaign in recent months which has more in common with the run-up to a general election than with the process of making decisions by a Christian community. While full-page advertisements, articles, letters and leaders in the press, debates on radio and television, booklets and letters galore through the letter box, pre-Synod polls, threats by one side or the other, and the citing of voting figures in deaneries and dioceses to support a particular line, may all contribute to the right decision in the end, they do not appear to have led even this part of the Body of Christ to a consensus, which is something that cannot be defined solely in mathematical terms and certainly not 68 per cent of votes in deanery synods. It is only that consensus, I believe, which allows us to claim to know the will of God and which alone can justify a momentous break with the tradition of the Church, a tradition which has been held from the beginning and which is still held by the majority of Christian people.

Nor is it appropriate to suggest that credibility in the eyes of the world demands that we go ahead. I am not aware of any passage in the gospels which would support such a demand, but I am very conscious of Our Lord's warnings that his followers would be widely persecuted and despised if they remained true to him. The seeking of even acceptability, let alone popularity, in the face of public opinion has enormous dangers for the integrity of the Church. Nor does it gain either respect in the long term or lasting conversions to Jesus Christ.

This is God's Church, not ours, and until I am convinced that he has led all of us together in the Church of England into radical change I must vote against it. As I do so I shall be aware that the Cross which is the symbol of our faith is a different shape from the cross on a ballot paper.

Mrs Kate Griffiths (Gloucester): In the majestic nave of Durham Cathedral, set in the stone floor, right across the far back, is a line of blue marble. Beyond this line in the Middle Ages no woman was allowed to pass. Some of the arguments and undertones in this present controversy seem to me to be as alien to the Christian Gospel as that line of blue marble. For example, there seems to be stalking abroad in parts of the Church the idea, incomprehensible to me, that whereas male sexuality and homosexuality are acceptable to God, female sexuality is in some way reprehensible. On the interpretation of Holy Scripture, I do not always find the transposition of a particular set of circumstances into a general principle convincing, especially when this is done on a selective basis. Thus if the fact that Our Lord chose only male disciples is conclusive evidence of the divine ordering of clergy in the Church of England today why do we not insist that since only male disciples were present at the Last Supper only men should partake of Holy Communion? In the light of other Scripture, I do not fully understand (and I am glad to hear that neither do some scholars) the references to men and women, headship, authority and teaching in 1 Corinthians and 1 Timothy; but if their relevance for this business today is as clear as opponents of this motion believe, their battle would have been fought and won long ago and there would be no teaching and preaching role for women in the mission field, no women Readers, no women deacons, no women lay members of Synod, no woman Prime Minister and no Queen allowed to be Supreme Governor of the Church of England.

As for the argument that we should wait until permission is given by the Church of Rome, Rome does not recognise even our male clergy, and its own teaching is that clergy should be not only male but celibate.

Like many in the Church of England who have not been campaigners on either side, I have been tempted to abstain, but the arguments on either side have now been rehearsed at such great length that abstention is simply not good enough. Our Lord prayed that we might be one, that the world might believe. I cannot believe that this prolonging of public polarisation is in the cause of the Gospel. So I shall vote for the motion, but with this caveat (or two or three caveats).

We need to remember and reinstate in our Church life, in our theological colleges, in our leadership, in our ministry to the nation, the major biblical, spiritual and doctrinal emphases and insights. Our salt has lost its tang. In so many leading clerical statements the emphasis seems to be on so-called political correctness, yet personal religious conviction, which is the only sure footing of the social gospel, is belittled and at a discount. We are hearing a lot about priests; where in the Church of England is there room for a prophet? Would he pass a selection board? Would his theological college be closed down? Would he be licensed to preach? Would Crown Appointments make him a bishop? If so, how would a prophet fit in with the fashionable but unscriptural idea of episcopal collegiality? Finally, if this Measure is passed it must not be implemented in an illiberal way. Promises are not enough. We must in the Church of England find room again for the prophet. We had a warning about this in a recent Crockford preface, about the potential illiberality of a monochrome liberal establishment. I believe that the only way to safeguard against this is to retain some independent theological colleges and to ensure in future that a diocesan bishop and his suffragan always come from different theological backgrounds and traditions. *(The Chairman rang the bell.)*

Mrs Anne Ellis (Exeter): When the bishop comes to a parish to institute a new vicar, the archdeacon, who has a walk-on part (or perhaps one should call it a walk-about part) reads these words at the beginning of the service: 'The Church of England is part of the one holy catholic and apostolic Church, worshipping the one true God, Father, Son and Holy Spirit.' That sounds fine but is it true? And if it is true, what constraints does it put us under today? The Oxford Apostles of the last century, did they weave a web of fantasy over the Church of England in declaring that it was part of the universal Church, or did they bring to life a forgotten but nevertheless uncomfortable truth? His Grace of Canterbury will forgive me, I am sure, if I say that we are not our own show, we are not even just a part of the total number of believers in Christ, we profess by our own articles of faith to belong to a Church that is both Catholic and apostolic.

On many matters this should not constrain us. There was an attempt to suggest that this matter was such and that women's ordination could slip into this category. In view of the ink spilt and controversy engaged upon over the past years, it would be a brave man who would now claim that this was a subsidiary issue; indeed the House of Bishops has told us what it is in its second report. So this is a big matter of big moment, for it illustrates in a way that could not be clearer that faith and order in the Christian Church are always gloriously intertwined. The ministry is part of the Christian Gospel and not just a vehicle for it. The reason why many of us will vote against the legislation is that it embarks on a new form of Anglicanism. Archdeacon Silk used the phrase 'government by provincial autonomy', where synods will decide on fundamental issues of faith and order without reference to the wider Church or, more exactly, without heeding the wider Church.

I was fortunate in the summer to be in a party making a pilgrimage to Rome and Assisi. At night in St Peter's Square the new floodlighting that lights up the dome of St Peter's casts into shadow the Michelangelo figures of the Apostles. They stand on either side of Our Lord and the Virgin as witnesses to the Resurrection and as foundation stones of the Church of God. Their presence is a reminder that the ordained ministry is not just a device to enable the laity to do their Christian work more effectively perhaps; Christian priesthood reflects the particular relationship that was special to the Twelve, and both the Scriptures and the traditions of the Church have emphasised that principle in confining the priesthood to men.

The legislation now before us claims in its opening words 'It shall be lawful for the [Church of England] to make provision [for the ordination of women as priests]'. If it receives Royal Assent, it will be lawful according to the law of the land, but whether it is lawful according to the law of the Church Catholic and apostolic is another matter. It is not open to us to tamper radically with that which is not exclusively ours. Because this legislation proposes to do precisely that, it is unacceptable to the Church of England.

If God had not been born in Palestine, if he had not been born male, if he had not chosen men to be his followers, if he had not chosen Peter to be the rock nor James to lead the Church . . .?

Today's vote is not just about Anglican orders, it is about the faith that we profess.

Mrs Shirley-Ann Williams (Exeter): I come not brandishing an axe like Mr Geldard but flourishing a spade. My metaphor is taken from Scripture. I look at the parable of the talents. What happened to the poor person who buried the one talent, hoping that it would stay the same, the same value, the same forever? We all know that when he dug it up there it was, a little muddy, a little dusty, perhaps the currency had changed. It had not grown. It had not done him any good. I believe that the parable is telling us something about the ministry of the people of this Church, particularly women.

We have all received many letters and heard many heart-rending stories (and been sent some pamphlets which do not do much credit to our Church, but I am not going to talk about those, the gospel of fear with which we have been bombarded, but about the gospel of hope) from ordinary people through the country, people who are looking forward to a Church that will move into the mission of the 1990s and the next century. This is not just a debate about the ordination of women to the priesthood for the sake of the women who are hoping, as June Osborne so movingly described, to have their vocation tested, it is about the ordinary people of the Church, the majority of people, who wish to be able to choose to experience the ministry of God's people, male and female. One letter I had said that on All Saints' Day 'we worshipped Our Lord and worshipped the saints, living and dead, who come in all shapes, sizes, colours and gender. Gifts and talents must be shared like loaves and fishes to feed the needy.' There are the parishes who say that 'we have had the ministry of a woman deacon for several years, and she now is to us our vicar. On a Sunday we have to have a priest whom we do not know to do those special bits of the sacrament, and our woman deacon cannot perform them. We would like to see her able to do that. We have been talking about unity with Rome; let us think about unity with the Free Churches. In our theological colleges we train women for the ministry where they are able to perform the sacramental acts. Again from a group of parishes in an ecumenical arrangement, we hear of the pain and sorrow of people when visiting women from other Churches can administer Holy Communion but when it is their own woman minister's turn to take the service she has to employ a visiting male priest whom they do not know.

So for the sake of the laypeople in the Church I would say: look at the figures, the voting is overwhelmingly in favour. Even if this does not go through today the voting is still overwhelmingly in favour, it is something that will not go away. It is not a set of people trying to fight a holy war, for if we talk in terms of a holy war that is what we will have, a holy war. I think that we need to talk in terms of development, mission, seeking the way that God is leading us. Change is inevitable. If change had never taken place we would all be back in the dark ages, long before Christianity. We must seek change and handle it in the way that God is showing us and leading us, and prayerfully accept what so many of us believe is the next stage forward in his Church.

Rt Hon John Selwyn Gummer MP (St Edmundsbury and Ipswich): Like a number of others, during the past weeks and months I have had very great cause to think what it is I would most miss if I were no longer able to be a member of the Church of England. Of course it is possible to talk of the services and the Prayer Book and the churches, but above all I know that it is our comprehensiveness. I was brought up in an Evangelical household, and my faith is fundamentally scriptural and my belief is firm because I believe in the revelation of God to man in a particular way. I may have moved from that in its expression to understand the fullness of the Catholic understanding of the faith, but I could not do that except in the Church of England because both those understandings are here. Very movingly earlier on a deacon asked us to give her the chance to test her vocation. My problem with this legislation is that under its terms we can only give her the chance to test her vocation if we remove the opportunity of vocation from many who hold orthodox views and who are now able to be part of the witness of the Church of England.

I am agnostic as to whether women can be priests, but I am deeply believing that the Church of England has a real role to play, not only in unity but in the Decade of Evangelism. I hate the fact that we have wasted all these years arguing about this instead of winning souls for Christ. That must be our common concern. But we do not get out of it by saying that it is so inevitable that we must accept it and that we do not need to care about the damage that it does to the unique statement of Anglicanism. It is not the same as what happened at the Reformation, for then we sought to recover truths that had been lost, we did not claim that we had new truths which we alone could pass on to the Church. We sought to get rid of accretions which had accumulated, we did not insist that membership of the Church, vocation within the Church, full communion in the Church, depended upon the acceptance of something which has never been accepted for two thousand years and which cannot be seen as rooted and grounded in Scripture.

I therefore turn to my Evangelical friends. One great thing has come from these discussions and it is shown not only in our common feeling about Oak Hill and Mirfield but in so many other areas. What we have learned is that our commitment to Scripture and to the revealed Word of God is too important to allow us to deny the other's place in the Church. We must not dam either stream up. The Archbishop of Canterbury said that God calls us to take the risk of faith. I believe that the risk of faith is that he has asked us to stand firm by his word until we know that it is his time to proclaim a different Gospel in a different way with a different ministry from that which we have had for two thousand years. That time is his time. Our risk of faith is to say to the world, 'It's not when you tell us to do it, it's when we know that God has told us to do it.'

The Bishop of Ely (Rt Revd Stephen Sykes): I would like to follow that remark by warning Mr Gummer that he will find in the Roman Church an even greater comprehensiveness than exists in the Church of England.

I want to speak of the real Roman Church which matters to me very much, as do my relations with the Orthodox Churches. It is true, as the Bishop of Birmingham has said, that there is official opposition to our proposal, and their arguments must be taken very seriously. It is not true that for the Roman Church this subject is closed and that discussion is impossible.

More than a year ago I attended a meeting of the international Roman Catholic periodical *Concilium* in Louvain, and I was besieged by groups of Roman Catholics from France, from Germany, from Belgium, from Holland, urging me to support this legislation. That is not the view of an irresponsible group of mavericks. In an article published in 1969 in *Sacramentum Mundi* on the subject of orders and ordination, the distinguished Belgian Jesuit Piet Fransen wrote that the issue of the ordination of women 'does not appear to be a dogmatic question'. It is, he said, a matter of ' "ecclesiastical economy" which being pre-eminently pastoral should be given a solution . . . adapted to the situation of Christian people in a given region'. Let us not talk too glibly of provincial autonomy. That was very severely criticised at the last Lambeth Conference. We are an interdependent Church and we belong to one another; it is responsible, in such an interdependent Church, for a Church in one context to take a certain decision which is not taken by Churches in all other contexts. I would add to my quotation from *Sacramentum Mundi* that that volume, published, as I say, in 1969, carried both the *nihil obstat* and the *imprimatur*.

Even after the publication of the statement *Inter Insigniores* in 1977 a French Dominican, Christian Duquoc, clearly articulates in his book *Provisional Churches* his opposition to a theology which fights for social and political equality of women and men but which then maintains that it only applies spiritually within a Church in which men are to rule, creating – and he was highly critical of this – a *cordon sanitaire* round the priesthood in a way which, he argued, was profoundly uncatholic.

That is the real Roman Catholic Church. As the leading article in this week's *Tablet* shows, it is perfectly possible to consider these arguments in a Catholic context without pretending that what is called Catholic faith and order is about to collapse or that our sacraments are about to become doubtful or invalid.

I would like to tell Synod how much I affirm the truth that the argument in favour of this proposition rests upon a theological grasp of the doctrines of Trinity, Incarnation and Atonement which lie at the heart of our faith. I am truly sorry that the circumstances of our debate prevent me from developing that in a fully theologically responsible way, but I would like to leave Synod with the clear message that it is not fashion, it is not civil rights, it is not the drive for self-fulfilment which undergirds the proposition among those of us who support it, but it is faithfulness to the doctrines of the Trinity and Incarnation, to our Anglican tradition which permits us to judge, as Richard Hooker said, of times and seasons, that 'now is a new grown occasion' when churchpeople may affirm the proposal before us as fully consistent with the faith of the one holy catholic and apostolic Church.

Canon Christopher Colven (London): Like many members, I spent last night praying. I placed myself at the foot of the Cross, asking for discernment, asking God to make clear his will for our part of his Church. In my prayer I kept being led back to the first chapter of the first letter to the Corinthians, where Paul is deeply concerned about the factions within the Corinthian Church and how their divisions have become open scandal, hindering the spread of the Gospel. His plea for reconciliation and for a new beginning is based not on any human logic but solely on the atoning death of Jesus Christ: 'The language of the Cross may be illogical to those who are not on the way to salvation but those of us who are on the way see it as God's power to save.'

I represent the diocese of London in this Synod and, I suppose, because I live centrally the media have pursued me over the past few days. In many of the interviews there have been the same underlying questions which I know have been of concern to many Synod members as they have to me. If this legislation does not gain its necessary majorities will we lose credibility with the rest of our society? Will the ordinary people of our country find our decision hard, if not impossible, to comprehend? Will it be yet another barrier to evangelism? A woman Prime Minister, female judges: why does the established Church not get its act together? Those questions are not easy to answer, unless one brings them before Scripture and the witness of 1 Corinthians, where Paul teaches us that here we are, preaching a crucified Christ, to the Jews an obstacle they cannot get over, to the pagans madness, but to those who have been called, whether Jews or Greeks, a Christ who is the power and the wisdom of God, for God's foolishness is wiser than human wisdom and God's weakness is stronger than human strength.

I hope that as I stand here I do not have too many hang-ups about women's ministry. It would not worry me, for instance, if the functions of my own archdeacon were given over to a woman tomorrow, and the person who taught me most about Christ and about prayer was an elderly recluse. I believe that we have neglected feminine insights for too long, greatly to our impoverishment as a Church. Yet before the Cross last night I saw with a greater clarity than ever before that we as Christ's witnesses must not be afraid to stand over and above contemporary wisdom, for we are called not to conform to the secular agenda and expectation but to challenge its presuppositions, and our voice should ever be a prophetic one, goading women and men towards the salvation held out for them in Jesus Christ.

The questions that we should ask ourselves are not about whether our decisions accord with received wisdom in society but whether they do justice to the revelation of Jesus Christ in the Gospel. Is the unbroken tradition of Scripture and Christian practice through two thousand years part of the prophetic will of Christ, not just for the ordering of his Church but for the authentic differentiation of male and female? Is this part of God's apparent foolishness which is in reality wiser than any human wisdom? I am honestly not sure. I am not one of those who can say, 'No, not ever', I just do not know; but I suspect, I feel intuitively, deep within my heart, that in Christian priesthood we touch a mystery which as yet we cannot fully articulate but which nonetheless remains as a disquieting challenge to us at the end of this century as it has done for two thousand years. A crucified Christ may be an obstacle to some, and madness to others, but the witness of Scripture is that the Cross is the way to salvation. The maleness of Christian ministerial priesthood may also be an obstacle to some and madness to others, but I have yet to be convinced that it is not part of God's revelation for the salvation of us all.

Revd Dr Paul Avis (Exeter): We are told that the outcome of our decision today is particularly close in the House of Laity. Before coming to Synod I asked a rather different House of Laity to vote on this issue. My House of Laity consisted of a primary school assembly of a hundred boys and girls aged 5-11. I asked them, 'Why does the Church not have women priests and vicars?' and the answer came back from those youngsters, 'Because Jesus chose twelve men.' Question: 'Why did Jesus choose only men?' Answer: 'Because in those days women stopped at home, looked after the children and did the housework.' Question: 'If Jesus were here today and looking for twelve helpers, would he choose only men, or would he choose women as well as men to help him?' Answer: 'He would choose them half and half; only that would be fair.' I asked for a show of hands, and 95 out of the 100 present voted for women priests and vicars.

You may ask me what youngsters of 5-11 know about Scripture and tradition. I may in return remind you of the text that says 'Out of the mouth of babes . . .' That is important because they are our parishioners of the future –[*Several members:* Today.] They are our adult worshippers of the future, shall I say?

It is a strange paradox that some Anglican Catholics and some Anglican Evangelicals who disagree about so much that they believe to be fundamental should combine to oppose the ordination of women priests, though they do so for different and, to some extent, opposed reasons. This is perplexing for a Church like ours which regards itself as both Catholic and Reformed, which has its roots in the structures of the ancient undivided Church, with its sacraments, creeds and episcopate, yet which purged itself of abuses and corruptions in the light of the Gospel at the Reformation. So some say that because we are Catholic we cannot do this thing, and others say that because we are Reformed we cannot do this thing. I want to say that because we are both Catholic and Reformed we have the right and the duty to do this thing.

What does it mean to be Catholic? Does it mean being patriarchal and hierarchical? Does it mean that we must take our cue from other Christian communions rather than from our own conscience and judgment? Does it mean that when we see an urgent pastoral need we cannot act? That was not the line taken at the Reformation. Then it was affirmed that a branch of the Catholic Church had the right and duty to reform itself, including its ministry. Catholicity is to do with the integrity and wholeness of the Church, in which all humanity is included and represented and the hopes and aspirations of all human beings may be fulfilled. The catholicity of the Church, in my view, is not impaired one half so much by its existence in separate communions as it is by debarring women from the sacred ministry. Catholicity must mean that a Church contains all that is necessary to regulate and conduct its life, for the fullness of Christ through the Holy Spirit indwells the Church. Catholicity does not belong to one branch of the Church more than to another, it is an attribute of every branch of the Church. It abides through change, development and reform. The English Church is Catholic today and will be equally Catholic when she has women priests. In fact, her catholicity will be enhanced because she will be more fully inclusive and representative of all humanity redeemed in Christ.

The Bishop of Newcastle (Rt Revd Alec Graham): I have scrapped the speech which I had written. I had intended to offer four good Anglican reasons, as I understood them, for saying no, but members have heard them all before, and put better than I can. It was the Bishop of Guildford's speech which moved me to abandon my own for he made some points which I venture to say deserve to be questioned. He will forgive me for speaking plainly. I hope I heard him correctly and that I quote him correctly.

He stated, if I heard him aright, that Scripture is inconclusive on the matter of the ordination of women. Surely Scripture never addresses that question? As far as I recollect, that precise question is never addressed. Then he claimed that the ordination of women to the priesthood is consonant with Scripture. We all know that to be a matter of opinion. There is argument enough about that, as we all know.

Then he claimed that it was required by tradition. That really is quite a claim. He conceded that ordination of women to the priesthood is not required by tradition in the sense that it has never happened before, but tradition is not just doing what has always been done before, an ever heavier load of practices and prohibitions. The Bishop maintained that ordination of women to the priesthood is demanded by the truth, required by the truth, as it has been handed down to us. If he had said it was demanded by the contemporary world, that is certainly often maintained and, we should all agree, is arguable, but surely it is not correct to say that tradition requires this development, for in this context tradition is the expression of the mind of the Church as set down in Scripture, interpreting, moulding, shaping the understanding of Scripture and of the mind of God revealed there, influenced by the contemporary world, tested by mind and conscience and tested against the original deposit. Tradition is set forward by the interplay between Scripture, the received mind of the Church, today's world and today's church members. That I understand to be the nature of tradition in this context. Surely it is quite misleading to enlist tradition without qualification in favour of this legislation, for it is at this very point that the arguments in favour of the legislation are at their weakest. I hope that the Synod will not be beguiled by the Bishop of Guildford in this respect, for he begs the question whether this is a legitimate development of the tradition at this stage in our Church's life. The answer to that, I submit, is either 'not proven' or a straight 'no'.

Dr Ruth Etchells (Durham): I want to go back to that blue marble line at the back of Durham Cathedral, beyond which women were not allowed to pass in the thirteenth and fourteenth centuries. Those who ruled this, those who so understood the place of women in the Church as literally only just inside the door, were our forefathers in the faith, belonging to the same Church, declaring the same creed and worshipping the same Lord as ourselves. They were part of that tradition for which we have a rightful care and they marked a particular point of understanding within it. Since then our understanding within that same tradition has broadened and deepened over the centuries, and women have moved forward in that cathedral into the pews in the nave, to the lectern, even to the pulpit, and recently into the choir as servers and assisting in administering Holy Communion, all in the name of the same faith which had earlier kept them far off.

However, there is still metaphorically a blue marble line round the altar itself, and it was this picture which came into my mind when I was working recently on some Bible studies on the epistle to the Ephesians, and I came to that marvellous verse 'Now in Christ Jesus you who were far away have been brought near by the blood of Christ'. It hit me with something of the force of a conversion experience that this tremendous statement of the full power and effect on divided people of the grace of Jesus Christ is as applicable to us today in this division in the Church, between men and women, as it was when it was written to that equally deep birthright division between Jews and non-Jews and their status within the early Church itself, for there was not by then an argument as to whether non-Jews should be admitted to the early Church but with what status. The struggle then was whether there should be two categories of citizenship in the Kingdom, those who by birth into God's holy race had reserved spiritual rights in the Church and those who had not because not so born. Today the struggle is whether there are those who, because of their birth into a particular sex, have certain reserved spiritual rights in the Church and those who have not because they are not so born. That passage in Ephesians, which is echoed in spirit all over the New Testament, declares the Gospel of Jesus Christ to be quite otherwise. It declares that through his grace that spiritual difference has, in his baptised people, been simply wiped out, the dividing wall destroyed, because his purpose was to create in himself one new being out of the two.

When I got to that point I realised with a force I had never realised before that for me this issue about women is about redemption, it is about a conviction of the adequacy of the saving work of Christ. Is the dividing wall of gender not susceptible to the same marvellous grace which could and did wipe out that deepest of divisions between a holy people and the rest? Could Christ redeem Gentiles but not gender?

I have come to believe that as long as there are areas of the Church's work and life which are closed to any group purely because of their birth we are putting into question the full efficacy of Christ's work on the Cross. I do not believe that we dare set limits on that redemption, and to close off areas of the Church's life is to do just that. If Christ's work for us all is not total it is nothing. We have to answer to Christ today, to Christ, not, though we care about them, to the rest of the Anglican Communion nor any other part of the universal Church. (*The Chairman rang the bell.*)

Mrs Sara Low (St Albans): When I was converted to Jesus Christ in my early twenties and came into the Church of England, I was told by my first parish priest, now a bishop on these benches, that the Church of England based itself on Holy Scripture, holy tradition and human reason. This legislation gives me the gravest possible concern on all three counts.

One of the things that I have learned in my time as a Christian is that where we are faithful to the revealed truth, there the promises of the New Testament are fulfilled. The Churches that believe this and do it are, in my experience, those that are blessed.

Like many of those here, I have listened for nearly twenty years to this debate. I listened very carefully to the early arguments about Jesus's cultural conditioning and the claim that Jesus did not have the freedom to appoint women. If cultural conditioning was determinative for Jesus then all his teaching and all his actions are thus heavily influenced. We are no longer talking about the eternal Son of God. Jesus Christ is different today from what he was yesterday, and he will be different again tomorrow. I have listened to the arguments that the early Church was equally unable to make this change yet, on the contrary, what could have made a bigger bridgehead with the pagan world than the introduction of women priests, with which they were already familiar? I have listened to arguments on St Paul where one classic quotation has been wrenched out of context, given a meaning that no previous generation of believers has given it, and seen it used to deny the clear teaching on headship in the rest of St Paul's letters. I have listened to the doctrine of creation being divided into greater and lesser truths, so that the complementarity of male and female has been debased to a banal interchangeability. I have listened patiently to talk of prayerful, thoughtful majorities when surely our problem is that the minority is also prayerful and thoughtful.

These are not comfortable things to say, but they must be said because if the Synod overturns scriptural authority today it will be no good coming back next time and hoping to impose it on other issues. For the Church, the authority of the Scriptures and the example of Jesus have always been determinative; I do not believe that this House has the authority to overturn them.

My second concern is the legislation itself. What of those who dissent? It seems strange, does it not, to call those who faithfully believe what the Church has always believed 'dissenters'? Bishops and archbishops may give verbal assurances that there will be no persecution against such priests and laypeople, but it is with great sadness that I have to tell the bishops that I have not met one opponent of the Measure who believes them. The reasons are simple. First, no verbal assurance can undo the fact that you are legislating for two classes of Christian; any good intentions that may exist will wither before the law and practice, as in other provinces. Second, in many dioceses the spirit of this legislation has been in operation for some years. Orthodox clergy are excluded from appointments and orthodox laity are made to feel excluded from that warm glow of official approval, as if they were suffering from some embarrassing handicap. I have experienced that myself often enough in these corridors.

However, if the human injustice of this legislation, which eases old men into retirement and condemns others to serve forever under authorities whose primary qualification is compromise, is disgraceful, it is as nothing besides its theological arrogance and blasphemy. The legislation clearly instructs the Lord God Almighty whom he may raise up to lead the Church. The Holy Spirit will be told, 'You may choose anyone you want so long as it is one of us.' A Church that denies the sovereignty of God is no longer a Church. The fruits of this debate are not the fruits of the Holy Spirit.

What of tomorrow? If you wake in the morning having voted yes, you will know that you have voted for a Church irreconcilably divided, for whom the revealed truth of God is no longer authoritative. If you vote no, you will wake to tears and a healing ministry, but above all to the possibility of a renewed New Testament Church, for all of us could then be united in encouraging, training and funding the ministry of priest, deacon, teacher, prophet, healer, administrator, spiritual director – all promised by the Holy Spirit.

I urge Synod to vote for the authority of the Word of God, for the unity of Christ's Church and against this ruinous legislation.

Revd Pete Broadbent (London): It is a strange experience, is it not, that we are sitting here with a dual agenda. We are conscious of the fact that we are being watched by the world round us, and many of us have come here with people saying to us, 'Go on, go for it.' I was at a party last Friday with many friends who are not Christians and who were amazed that we had actually got this far but were urging us towards it. Yet we are also conscious that we cannot make that decision based on the urgings of the world outside.

It is slightly strange that in the debate so far we have heard many folk from the opposition trying to claim that revelation and adherence to Scripture and to tradition are all on their side and that those of us who want the legislation to go through are those who do not care about the tradition or about wrestling hard with what Scripture says. I want to bear witness to the fact that those of us from the Evangelical side who have come to this particular stage and want to vote for the legislation have done so with lots of hard work.

I was going through my files earlier on, preparing for this debate, and I dragged out a speech that I had made at theological college in the 1970s in which I argued very strongly against the ordination of women to headship because at that stage in my pilgrimage I still believed that those headship texts worked. It was not until I got to my first curacy, where I began to work through the issues, that I recognised that the texts demanded more hard work and I changed my opinion.

The thing that we need to do, particularly those of us who are Evangelicals, is to ask seriously: does headship, which has been a determining factor in the way we have addressed these issues, bear the weight which people give to it? (I apologise to those members who think of the priesthood as representative — they can switch off for a few minutes, if they have not done so already! This is not their agenda.) Those of us who want to be faithful to the matter of headship and ask where it leads us must ask whether it has the power and the capacity to determine the way in which our ministry goes and therefore to rule out the ordination of women to the priesthood. I think that headship dies the death of a thousand qualifications. As you look at it and realise that the texts do not bear that weight, you have to change your mind. Christina Baxter has already looked at some of the theological issues; I want to say that when you look at the practicalities of headship it does not seem to work.

First, those who argue for headship as leadership in creation — and that is where the Timothy texts take you — then begin to backfire when they realise what it means, because they exclude from their argument leadership in political and national life. It is OK for women to be in headship, but only in national life and politics; there is something different about the Church and about marriage, and headship is male there. If you are arguing from creation, you cannot sustain that ambiguity. Headship must be male throughout the whole of creation, according to the texts, or else it is disqualified from being that universal headship which is argued for.

There are also those from my side of the Church who argue that headship is equated with leadership and the teaching office; they have worked very hard to try to show that it is important that male leadership and male teaching are the way in which we should do our business in the Church still, and that we should preserve this; but when you ask them about the great plethora of female theologians and female teachers in the Church and where their role is, and those who are authorised as Readers and as deacons to preach the word of God, they begin to haver. Yes, it is possible that we can have women teaching in Church, they say, but the point is that leadership and the teaching office must be the preserve of males at the main services. Where is that distinction in St Paul? It is not there.

Third, does your doctrine of headship equate with reality and practicality? Where do you exercise headship in your own lives? If you believe in headship in marriage and you are a male, when did you last exercise headship in your relationship? (*Laughter*) What does it mean? And if it means nothing in marriage, and it means very little in the Church, then perhaps it cannot bear the weight put on it and perhaps we need a different model, that of the servant, which Jesus brought us.

Mr Hugh Craig (Oxford): I could wish that we were now debating something that would release the talents of the 99 per cent of laywomen who will not seek ordination, some of whom we treat quite shabbily, that we were debating this subject from a common understanding of the nature of the ordained ministry or that we were considering new forms of ministry for women, of similar standing to those for men and tailored to their distinctive and unquestioned abilities. My own understanding of the New Testament – and I have read it as well as Pete Broadbent – and of those passages in particular that the advocates of the Measure tend to dismiss is that it teaches at the same time an equality of standing of men and women before God, together with the differentiation and complementarity of function which is wholly missing from this legislation and from the arguments advanced for it. My unease on this ground alone would persuade me to vote against the Measure.

However, even if we accept that women should be ordained to an identity of office with men, is the method before us acceptable? Surely such authorisation should be given in as generous a way as possible to the women concerned, and it should be done in such a manner that those unhappy with the development can remain as full-hearted members of the Church co-existing with those who take the opposite view, just as both sides do now. I dislike, therefore, the safeguard that an existing bishop can refuse ordination on the grounds of gender alone to a woman if the Church at large has sanctioned such ordination; and I dislike the view of the House of Bishops in GS 764 on which this legislation is based which explicitly states that after the passing of the Measure they would regard as anomalous the appointment of a bishop who was, in effect, opposed to the Measure. Answers given to Questions, including those last night, as to whether the House of Bishops really means this have confirmed that it does.

While the legislation itself is silent on the point, amendments moved by me to make explicit that opponents who were prepared to work the system should not be denied preferment were resisted by the revision committee, the members -in-charge and the Synod. The legislation itself differentiates between present and future bishops, clearly indicating that a change in the nature of the episcopate is expected. I find it a trifle disingenuous that some bishops are now saying that they would be happy for opponents to be appointed while the formal decision of their House to the contrary remains unrescinded.

We know that we are divided on this issue roughly two to one. If one-third of the Church find that their clergy are refused preferment, their ordinands rejected, that one-third, laity as well as clergy, will in due course reluctantly be forced to the conclusion that they have no place in a Church that denies them access to ministry, to preferment and to the episcopate; and there is evidence from appointments, from selection conferences, from our own Appointments Sub-Committee, that the policy of GS 764 is already at work – there is a whiff of it in the unsatisfactory report that we will debate tomorrow.

I am conscious that the majority of churchfolk have voted for these Measures to be passed. My own careful canvass of about half the Oxford lay electors shows that about 15 per cent passionately want the Measure and about 11 per cent passionately do not. Compare that with the about 2 per cent of genuine constituents who have written to me to see the highly orchestrated postal campaign in its proper perspective. The other 74 per cent range from mostly mild approval to mild disapproval, with some wishing that we would simply talk about something else. I fail to detect in any of that 74 per cent a desire for the division that this legislation with GS 764 will entail; laity know that we need that like we need a hole in the head. We ought to have legislation less concerned about those who leave and more generous to the great majority of the opponents who would wish to stay. Dissentients who are prepared to live and let live in the Church without concealing their view that the Church might have made a mistake should be shown the same consideration as those who take the opposite view. It would be administratively less tidy, pastorally sound, workable, hold us together and minimise secession. Such option the present Measure does not offer and the members-in-charge have specifically rejected. In the name of charity and unity it needs to be reconsidered; in its present form approval for this Measure should be refused.

The Chairman: I am told that there was a fire in the Vitello d'Oro, but a very small one, and it will not affect lunch!

(Adjournment)

The Archbishop of Canterbury (Dr George Carey) *took the Chair at 2.30 p.m.*

LEGISLATIVE BUSINESS

Draft Priests (Ordination of Women) Measure (GS 830C)

(Resumed debate)

Professor David McClean (Sheffield): There are many in the Church and outside it who wonder at the subtle and convoluted arguments with which we address a simple question: are the gifts which God has given to women acceptable in his service in the office of priest? I believe, with most members of the Church of England, that the answer is yes and that we shall remove today the man-made legal obstacles to the ordination of women to the priesthood, not to what David Silk called a provisional ministry but to the office of priest in the full sense of our canon law.

I begin with the simple recognition of the Church's need now, in our time and in our country, for women priests. Please let me not be misheard. I am not talking of secular priorities and secular values but of the imperative that we bring the Gospel of Jesus Christ to our neighbours. That task requires the talents, the insights, the skills of every one of us, male and female alike, and in it the ordained ministry has a critical role. So long as we refuse to allow women to play a full part in the work of ordained ministry we are squandering God's gifts and making the task of evangelism harder.

In this we Anglicans can speak from experience. To hear some of the speeches this morning one could imagine that the Synod was being asked to take a first step into wholly unknown territory, but women priests are an established part of Anglican experience in provinces from Canada to New Zealand, from Hong Kong to the United Kingdom in the Church of Ireland. In some of those provinces, yes, the arrival of women priests was controversial, but they now win wide acceptance. The Church of England is not being asked to take the role of a brave pioneer but to catch up with many of our Anglican brothers and sisters.

Many of us can remember the opposition to the idea that the Church of England should ordain women to the diaconate. I remember Father Geldard's warnings against the fundamental change that it entailed, of the tensions that it would create, of the ecumenical dangers, of the divisiveness of our action in the context of the Anglican Communion, but who would now reverse that decision? We have a woman deacon in my own parish; we think the world of her. We have found that her presence adds a special quality to the Church's ministry, a quality which would find full and proper expression in her ordination as a priest and in her presidency of the Eucharist. It is not because she wants it; it is a judgment that to ordain her and hundreds like her would better express the joyful, saving, redeeming Gospel than pronouncing her continued exclusion.

If women are to be ordained priest, how best does the Church bring about the change? That takes us to the actual legislation before us. I was amazed to hear it called 'legislation by stealth'; never has stealth been so public and open. I am getting rather tired of the allegation that the legislation is divisive and unfair and biased. The issue may be divisive but the clear purpose and intent of the legislation and of all those who contributed to its formulation is to preserve the unity of the Church. As to its supposed unfairness and bias, what lies behind those words is the argument that nothing is acceptable unless it treats with absolute equality the position that women should be eligible for the priesthood and the position that would exclude them; nothing less is acceptable, nothing less is just.

What, however, is the position today? Does the Church now give equal value to those two positions? Of course not. If it did we would not need today's debate. I am a lawyer and justice is central to my professional concerns. It saddens me greatly to hear a cry for justice used to defend injustice, a call for equal treatment used to perpetuate discrimination.

What about the way in which the legislation treats those, especially those who might be elected as bishops, who will remain unhappy about the priestly ordination of women? There is no provision in the legislation which bars such people from preferment, nothing which sets out to exclude or undervalue them. In looking at this issue, we must be very careful in our use of the documents produced in past years. Even the Bishop of London, in his moving speech this morning, quoted at length from a report written before the Synod spent two days in 1989 revising and improving the legislation, a report addressing a text other than the one now before us. More seriously, Mr Craig just before lunch repeated a serious misunderstanding of an even earlier 1987 report of the House of Bishops. It is true that the House of Bishops recognised that some people would be so fundamentally at odds with canon law as amended by this legislation that they could not serve as bishops, for sound theology, sound Catholic theology, I believe, emphasises that a bishop acts not for himself but for the Church in which he holds office, and he cannot be totally at odds with the canon law of that Church; but Mr Craig failed to cite a sentence in the self-same paragraph: 'Nonetheless in certain circumstances it may be that a diocese requests a bishop who is prepared not to ordain women to the priesthood', and the bishops went on to hope that the Crown Appointments

Commission would respect that position. Nothing in the legislation stands in the way. Clause 2 seeks not to marginalise but to offer some help.

What the legislation does more generally is to give its opponents, both clergy and laity alike, not mere assurances but legal rights, clearly stated and entrenched. That is something that no other Anglican province has attempted, so if there have been some unhappy situations in other provinces they arose in a different context from the one that we would create by this legislation. I have heard it today called dire, wretched, ruinous and even blasphemous, and no doubt the adjectives will continue to pile up, but I think that the Synod can take pride in the way it has expressed in this draft legislation its concern for the theological convictions and, if need be, the material welfare of those most hostile to it. We have here a realistic and a generous framework for the exercise of that sensitive leadership which the Church needs at a time of change.

Your Grace's predecessor, Lord Coggan, has reminded us that were the legislation to fail to get the required majorities today we would endure further years of distraction from our main task. That has been echoed in speeches that we have heard this morning. Endless debate merely drains the energies that are needed in the task of evangelism.

It has been for me and for my colleagues on the steering committee an enormous privilege to have been entrusted with the charge of this legislation, and we are so grateful to those who have sent us in recent days some very moving words of encouragement. We in our turn want to encourage the Synod. For too long the special gifts of women, gifts from a generous Creator God, have been under-used and under-valued. We have locked their talents away. We have refused to women the chance to respond to a call to use their gifts in lives devoted to the priestly ministry of Christ's Church. Today, this very afternoon, may we in this room take the marvellous opportunity that we have to unlock those gifts, to enrich the Church and to strengthen it in the service of God.

The Bishop of Sheffield (Rt Revd David Lunn): Deaf adders. That is what we have all become, deaf adders that stop their ears (Psalm 58). [*Several members:* Can't hear!] Deaf adders who want to unplug their earholes!

I love listening to David McClean, an honourable man like Brutus (but I am not being snide), a good man; we are proud of him in the diocese of Sheffield, and I am glad that he has just become our Chancellor, a thoughtful, learned, helpful man of the law — but sometimes deaf. Like so many of the enthusiasts for this legislation, deafer than your average adder. In Sheffield, ever in the forefront of modern progress, we have gone in for trams, supertrams, of course. Night and day the massive viaducts that will take these great beasts are being built, and the gossip is that there has been a terrible mistake: the lines are not going to meet. It conjures up a splendid picture of myriad trams chugging into eternity, never meeting, never coming back. Or perhaps — and is not this where we are? – that 'darkling plain where ignorant armies clash by night'. Our vote this afternoon must be a vote of the hearing and not of those who stop their ears.

There are two issues which came up a number of times this morning and on which we need hearing, un-deaf adders this afternoon: revelation and comprehensiveness. Revelation: forgive me for coming back to this. Forgive me too for being personal and anecdotal. I count it as an act of a kindly providence that I was born and brought up in Northumberland and came to faith in my teens in my local parish church, St George, Cullercoats, and that it was a church with a long Prayer Book Catholic tradition. We never doubted that our fellow Northumbrians, Bede and Cuthbert (it was not Cuthbert who put the blue line in Durham Cathedral) were fellow members of the same Church as us. We never doubted that it was concerning this same faith and same Church that Our Lord Jesus Christ after his resurrection gave commandment through the Holy Spirit to the apostles whom he had chosen (St Luke). We never doubted that the same faith had been preserved and handed on in the Scriptures of the New Testament. We never doubted that in the Prayer Book and Ordinal, despite the storms of the Reformation, almost by a miracle, perhaps by a miracle, this Catholic, apostolic and scriptural faith had been preserved within the Church of England. We never doubted that it was the faith once delivered to the saints (St Jude this time) that we were bidden to guard, to live and to hand on to others. It is in this a–liturgical, I suppose, sense that I was and am a Prayer Book Catholic and a northern Catholic.

The key words here are 'the faith once delivered to the saints'. Every time I use them in public a very learned priest of the diocese, a friend and contemporary of mine, writes to protest. He, like so many of my college contemporaries, has drunk deep of the poisoned well of Nineham and Lightfoot, of modern scholarship. He is becoming, or has become, one of those who believe that under the guidance of the Holy Spirit we – I quote, I believe, a bishop but I will spare his blushes – 'can draw out depths of insight in Scripture which are sometimes contrary to the surface meaning of the scriptural texts'. That must mean 'If you don't like what the Bible says, try looking at it upside down.' My guide is a good deal older than Nineham. Before 200 AD Irenaeus wrote in his great work *Against the Heresies*: 'The Lord gave his Apostles authority to preach the Gospel. Through them we have learnt the truth, that is the teaching of the Son of God. The Gospel which they then proclaimed they afterwards, by the will of God, handed down in writings.' The Bible accompanies the Church on its journey through the ages and to its eternal goal.

The supporters of the legislation are divided on this issue of revelation, perhaps more than they realise. Some (the majority, I suspect, though we have not heard much from them on this matter today), like my friend the learned parish priest, do not believe that there is a revelation with a given, known, tangible, authoritative content: the Holy Spirit leads us without embarrassing encumbrance from the past. Others, while believing in the reality of God's revealed truth, have convinced themselves that the revelation is silent on this 'indifferent' matter of ministry.

Oh, my deaf friends, hear me. If this legislation is approved this afternoon the authority of Scripture in the decision-making processes of the Church of England will have been inexorably and fatally weakened.

Let me speak particularly to the House of Bishops. The bishops are appointed to be the guardians of that faith once delivered to us. To me it is both astonishing and distressing that the first fruits of the coming to prominence of so many Evangelicals among the bishops has been the steady carrying forward of this profoundly — at best — a-scriptural and very probably unscriptural legislation. All of you, laywomen, laymen, deacons, presbyters, bishops, who believe that there is a concrete reality in God's revelation of himself, and that this is guarded, lived and handed on in Scripture and in the life of the Church, must hesitate for a very long time indeed before you vote for this legislation which, however its supporters may decorate it with quotations from Scripture, has its roots in a very different system of belief.

'Comprehensive' is my second key word. Not only am I a Prayer Book Catholic, I am also a firmly broad churchman, not central or liberal — they can be as narrow-minded as Ian Paisley; and it is our commitment to a faith and order rooted in Scripture, the Prayer Book and creeds that creates space for breadth and even eccentricity, and I welcome both. I do not see, despite the words of Professor McClean, even more despite the words of the Archbishop of Canterbury, space within this legislation for those who are its opponents. It is no wonder that these words about generosity and caring and charity grate so much on us. I speak as a bishop. I love my diocese. Most days I like being bishop. I am blessed with colleagues energetic and able who very much want me to stay as bishop. I would like to stay as bishop. But I cannot believe with this legislation that it makes any sense at all for a diocese to have a bishop who cannot give his wholehearted consent to the new Canons. It just does not make sense. Not only do I feel — and I may be wrong — that I am being excluded from the Church and from the ministry of the Church by what is proposed, I sense too that that Prayer Book Catholic, Tractarian tradition within the Church, which has contributed so much and with which so many of us feel at home, will be isolated, marginalised and very unlikely to survive.

The new rule, as it were, affects first bishops, then ordinands. Already it is not easy for ordinands in many of our colleges and most of our courses to survive if they are not wholehearted supporters of the ordination of women to the priesthood. The Archbishops assure us that there will be no prejudice against ordinands who do not accept the ordination of women to the priesthood. If I can say so without disrespect, who do they think they are kidding? They can only speak for their own dioceses anyhow, and they are not immortal, alas. What of the future? I do not believe that if we pass this legislation there is a future within the Church of England for those who at present are opposed to it. Some ghetto parishes will be able to survive almost indefinitely, but that is all. The rest is fox and crow – perhaps I should say 'fox and rook', to avoid misunderstanding – the rest is fox and rook stuff. Once the poor bird has been gulled into opening his beak and has lost the meat, he may as well fly away. (*The Chairman rang the bell.*)

The Chairman imposed a speech limit of five minutes.

Sir Leslie Fielding (Chichester): After so many years of debate we have come to the final moment of truth. A lot of us find it a frightening moment, more especially because we are not discussing here equal opportunities for women in secular society, we are called upon to take a decision on holy things: what is the truth revealed in Scripture, which is a holy Scripture, not just any scribblings, and what it is legitimate to do to develop a ministry which is an apostolic one. I would welcome a more active and widespread ministry for women which would fully use their talents, but I cannot see it in the form of the present proposal nor support that proposal in the atmosphere which now prevails. I respect the personal integrity of those who are in favour of the legislation, but I have to say that the legislation clearly rests on assumptions which are not proven beyond reasonable doubt and which can be and are widely contested, legislation which I personally find slightly un-Anglican in what is really expected of new bishops and ordinands and in the kind of uncertain safeguards which are offered.

We must be humble and recognise that our General Synod is self-confessedly an imperfect instrument. One of the last acts of the last Synod was to call for a rethink – do members recall that? – of our structures and purposes. It may well be, after this legislation is settled one way or another, that the next act of this Synod will be to get on with that overhaul. We do some things well, very well – I think in particular of our debate in the last group of sessions about cohabitation; but I also recall another debate on feminist theology in which we were less sure of our footing, in which we felt ill informed and apprehensive and where we looked for a way out. Do we really think that this Synod is qualified to make irreversible and sweeping changes, ultimately mandatory on everyone, to the way in which the word of God and the ministry of Christ's Church have usually been understood? Such issues ought not to be decided by small majorities at the expense of large minorities. What is required is a shared concern. This is not the Agricultural Council of the European Community in Brussels, where John Gummer, with great skill, regularly joins his colleagues in making decisions by qualified majority voting on sluice gate prices for cereals and monetary compensatory amounts for sheep meat and limitations on subsidies for oilseed rape. What is required is a wholehearted and widespread consensus in which all of us, or almost all of us, can see the prompting of the Holy Spirit.

That kind of consensus clearly has eluded us. We are split here in this chamber and out in the dioceses and the deaneries. It is wrong to move on to the ordination of women against the entreaties of orthodox believers who, however misguidedly, represent what has always up to now been normative and central in the Church of England. I shall vote against, in penitence, for I think that we all share part of the blame for the way in which this issue has been handled, but in faith that sooner or later we shall find an appropriate ministry for women which satisfies them and all of us.

Sister Carol CHN (Religious Communities): Today, it seems to me, we have an opportunity to be good news. The vote is about enabling women to be ordained priests, but the resonances are much wider because it is about the interrelationship of women and men in and for God. The debate has been creative where it has made us think through essential matters of belief, e.g. the implications of the Incarnation for women. It would be unhelpful to deny that the debate has also exposed fears and antipathies, a lot of emotional and psychological energy. Under the title 'The Ordination of Women to the Priesthood' there is a very mixed agenda.

This may not be so attractive but it is very much of the human condition. Christianity is about the transformation of the human condition into the maturity of Christ, and Christ is the recapitulation of humanity, the new humanity, the undistorted image of what we, men and women, are called to become. The whole Christ is the body of women with men together, reconciled, transfigured, redeemed. Our work today will be good news if it helps the Church to be a sign of the reconciled, transfigured, redeemed society on earth.

The Church is home for those seeking their eternal fulfilment in God through Christ. Are our 'welcome home' signs distorted? A very intelligent young Christian woman said to me recently that a No vote today will confirm her intelligent young non-Christian women friends in the view that the Church is a patriarchal set-up, unaffirming and unwelcoming to women. The cost of conscience is not limited to those who are opposed; it is borne and has been borne already in a variety of ways, not least by those who feel a Gospel constraint to go forward. Therese of Lisieux has been mentioned today; she happens to be one of my great gospel exemplars — she carried a copy of the gospels with her always. It is not always known that Therese actually wanted to be a priest, so much so that as she lay dying she noted the fact that God was taking her home before the day when she would be old enough to become a priest - if she were a man.

It matters that the Church expresses the baptismal identity of women as fully as possible throughout its ministerial structures because we are a holy people, a royal priesthood. The vote today, I suppose, is about enabling women to share in the ordained expression of that royal priesthood in the Church of England. It really does seem to me that this will surely come sooner or later, and later, I think, could be more costly than sooner all round. Today is largely a debate about timing and, despite continuing division, it seems to me that on balance it would be best to go forward now. Whether we do or not, however, whether the vote is yes or no, we still have an overriding responsibility and privilege to be good news, and an essential part of good news is that God's positive purpose is at work in all circumstances. That has to be so: in all things God works together for good for those who love him, as we do.

Today and in the days ahead, can we and the Church of England respond to the Resurrection Spirit that will surely be at work through our best attempts and our worst mistakes? Will we be one more item of bad news in the media, or can we by grace be a sign of hope, a sign of the Kingdom, in the way we handle our task, in the result today and onwards? I make that challenge to myself as much as to anyone else. It is arguably the most important task before us today.

Revd Penny Martin (Durham): - deacon in the diocese of Durham. I will be speaking very briefly, not least because to address this Synod for the first time on such a day is inclined to take the breath away.

When we are listening for the voice of God and for our conscience, let us not be assailed by other people's fears about a divided Church. This is a matter which divides us, yes, but we were never promised otherwise. We are being offered this careful legislation as a creative and flexible way forward, a way in which we can be held together. As is now very clear, a No vote would be far more serious, far more destructive, than if people were to have the courage to change their minds and vote in favour. The balance of power is held, it seems, by just a very few who can alter the fate of the legislation. For every single vote against we know that there are at least two who believe that it should proceed. This we know from our deaneries and our dioceses. For every single one we know that there are many more in our Church of England congregations who believe that the time has come to ordain women as priests. More important still, in the towns and villages where we seek to announce and embody the Gospel of Jesus Christ, we know that for every single one who is agonising now there are more still who would be bewildered, bemused and betrayed if the Synod were not to assent to this way forward. This is why those who intend to vote against the legislation need to be willing to change to vote in its favour.

The Church that we all love is often referred to as our mother. I am a daughter and a mother too. It seems to me that today we are present at the crowning moment of long months of waiting and a steadily increasing readiness. It is almost as if a child is about to be born, with all the pain and promise which that inevitably involves. It rests here with us whether this child is born alive or not. Either way there will be more pain, but only if we can move forward together can it all be made worth while. The unity of our Church is important to all of us. We shall be held together as, with caution and with courage, we release all the promise of the potential of women priests, and this can happen today, not if we defeat the Measure but if we welcome it with open arms.

The Dean of St Paul's (Very Revd Eric Evans): We would all like to congratulate the Revd Penny Martin on that speech which was most sincere and moving, though I cannot really agree with it. Our Lord did pray for the unity of the Church, that we may be one, and this is what concerns a great number of us today. In speeches which have come from the bishops — the Bishop of London, the Bishop of Newcastle, the Bishop of Sheffield — and from others the point has been stressed that there is a danger of schism. It is very real. Most of us here love the Church of England. We believe in Anglicanism. There is a toleration about it, a genius, that enables us to have our differences; no matter what stables we come out of, we all try and run the course together, some faster than others but basically all in the same race; and I think we are in all love and charity with each other in that race. While I am on my feet, may I say a word of thanks to June Osborne for her speech? It was very moving. Here was a cry from the heart and a lot of us felt enormous sympathy with it.

Nevertheless, we are here today to vote on the legislation before us — that is why we are present — and I honestly think that this legislation divides us because it almost, you could say, makes schism legitimate. I want to ask Synod not to tear the Church of England apart. I am sure there are better ways. The ministry of women has developed enormously over the years. Some of us have been in the Synod perhaps longer than we should have been, but if anyone had said, say ten or fifteen years ago, that women would actually be voting members of the House of Clergy we would have thought it ridiculous, but we have moved a long way since then. (*Applause*) So be it!

I plead that we may, even at this late hour, look at this whole thing again, because I am sure that there is a better way forward than the present legislation.

It may be, of course, that the Spirit is going to cause us division. One does not know. One has to trust the Spirit. Yet I do not really believe that schism is the way forward, and even if we go into different lobbies I do not think that we will be quite the same again. In matters of faith and order and morals, when opinions are divided I believe that overwhelming weight must be given to the tradition of the Church, especially when that tradition is not contrary to Scripture — and I do not think that it has been made out to be contrary to Scripture — rather than to innovation. The fact that the Church may well go into schism against itself is to my mind a theological objection because schism is a theological matter. I hope that those who are wavering on this issue will remember that.

The Archbishop of York (Dr John Habgood): If I may pick up where the Dean of St Paul's left us with the legislation, it seems to me that it is part of the fate of the Church of England to have to try to express things which are essentially spiritual, theological and pastoral in legislative terms. As soon as you try to do that you find yourself in, I believe, false opposition. When the legislation arises, as this does, out of a prolonged and intense process of controversy, inevitably built into it are what one might call safeguards against a worst case scenario. We are constantly in the Church of England finding ourselves trapped in that kind of situation, and there is, alas, no way out of it except to recognise that when you are in the process of forming legislation you are almost always looking at the worst case and building in safeguards. When you actually have to work it, you turn back into the theological, spiritual and pastoral mode and behave like a more reasonable human being (with all due respect to Professor McClean!). What we will in the end be concerned with in this legislation if, as I hope, it passes is how we will work it. The Bishop of Sheffield has poured some scorn on talking about generosity and being nice to one another and so on, but in fact the Church is about generosity, it is about accepting one another in Christ, it is about the spirit and not about the letter. This is why this debate and the whole style and tone of it is so important for the future – and not only for our future but for the future of a society which is deeply divided, and we look outwards to a world which is deeply divided. If we as Christian people cannot recognise our differences, cannot find ways in which we can go on together, cannot accept that many of those differences will continue and be accommodated, then really what hope is there for our world? That is the kind of responsibility which rests upon us.

I come out of most of a lifetime in the ecumenical movement. One of the things that the ecumenical movement teaches you is that actually Christians are different, that there are different cultural ways of expressing the faith. If we just go back into our little cubbyhole and say, 'This is my tradition, Prayer Book Catholic, or whatever it may be, and nobody is going to have a look in at that at all, and nobody is going to criticise it in any way or do anything which might appear to threaten it', then we are locked in a form of Christianity which may be satisfying for us, but which is, looked at from an ecumenical, a world, perspective, appallingly narrow.

As Christians we ought not to be worried about differences. There have always been differences in the Christian Church. This is not because there is something wrong with Christianity, it is because the focus of our unity is Christ and we respond to Christ in different ways out of our different personalities, out of our different cultural traditions and in different ages. This does not mean that we cut loose from tradition, but it is always a developing tradition as we try to bring our allegiance to Christ, our theological understanding, into the context of where we are now. Faith is impoverished if we exclude tradition.

We have been asked if there could be bishops opposed to the ordination of women if this legislation goes through. Well, as Professor McClean has already answered, of course there could be, if we really want them, if dioceses decide that they want them. Dioceses have a say. What I cannot abide is the sort of conspiracy theory which imagines that behind this legislation people are plotting. Conspiracy theories always assume a far greater degree of cunning than most of us possess. Frequently I read in the newspapers about what I am supposed to have done, and I marvel at my own ingenuity.

Mrs Margaret Laird (Third Church Estates Commissioner, Ex-officio): I speak in my personal, not my official, capacity.

The *Times* obituary for Bishop Gerald Ellison commented that it was said of him that being a rowing man he believed that the only way to make progress was by facing backwards. Digital watches do not encourage us to look backwards or forwards, and so we lose sight of the historical perspective. We may be planning for the future but we cannot ignore the past, and in this debate, if we were to do so, we would be in danger of destroying the essence of the Church of England. We need to beware of certain 17th and 18th century historians who promoted their own interpretations of the Church of England, claiming that it was an innovation with unrestricted authority to determine its own faith and order. They distorted the intention of many of the original English reformers who wished to return to faith as revealed in Scripture and to the received traditions of the early Church. Bishop Gore defined the Church of England as an ingeniously devised organisation for defeating the objects it is supposed to promote, and this is exactly what this legislation would do. No longer would our Church's authority be limited to such obligations as can be confirmed by Scripture, which has always been the Anglican way of restricting dogma. Bishop Gore noted that when it comes to dogma we tend to run away from principle and to take the easiest way round the next corner; and this is precisely how we have approached this issue. Even the first step was expressed in the negative rather than in a clear and affirming statement which pointed the way ahead.

Second, this Measure, as others have said, would defeat our intention to maintain the historic ministry. Any violation of this causes disruption, as Wesley's actions demonstrated, for order reflects doctrine. It is the corporate acceptance of this ministry which holds our Church together. This will lead to anomalies, ambiguities and, I fear, to a Church which, forgetful of the rock from which she was hewn, will be uncertain of her authority, unclear about her doctrine and unsure about the validity of her ministry.

The historical perspective also throws light on the purpose of synods which, as Professor Henry Chadwick reminded us, should act as a brake, to uphold the apostolic faith and to settle disputes and not, as this Synod threatens, to cause further division. The rejection of this legislation could, like the rejection of the Covenant proposals, lead to positive results, to a serious consideration of the development of a distinctive and structured women's ministry. To vote No would neither deny the valuable work of women deacons nor restrict the growing influence of women. St Monica's influence upon St Augustine did not depend on priestly orders.

Finally, I turn to an unexpected historical source, a canonisation document of St Frances of Rome who was greatly respected by Church and State in the fourteenth century. It records how in a vision she received into her arms the Christ child and was asked to show him to the people of Rome, not, she was told, in the form of bread and wine but in the person of Christ himself. With such an understanding of the ministry of women this legislation would be unnecessary.

Mr Philip Lovegrove (St Albans): Like the Dean of St Paul's, I have spent half my lifetime as a member of this Synod, and it probably shows. In 1965 I was an Evangelical minority. I did not realise it until I got here, I thought I was a Christian. I have been in a minority. I have done it, I have seen it and I have the T-shirt. I had alongside me in those days Mr Craig. The fundamental disagreements in the Church of England scorched across the floor and our doughty, worthy protagonists were none other than Oswald Clark (he has his binoculars on me up there in the gallery) and Maurice Chandler, so precious little seems to change. What we found as a minority was exactly some of the fears that have been raised today: Mrs Chatterley's three Ms, mistrust, marginalisation and mayhem. Yes, I did turn up at Gerald Ellison's first Bishop's Council in Chester — that is where I came from. He wondered who the devil this was, this Evangelical peasant up against a kingly bishop; we got on pretty well after the first meeting.

In that situation one does obviously feel marginalised — one did. One does obviously feel mistrustful. After all, all the bishops, my friend Sheffield, were Prayer Book Catholics; there was not a single conservative, classical, definite, biblical Evangelical among them — that seems to be the phraseology. However, having come from that position — and I am a mild sort of person so I was not into Mrs Chatterley's mayhem (if you believe that, you will believe anything) — over a period of time one has experienced in the Church of England the toleration that the Dean of St Paul's spoke about, and over that period of time, with constructive engagement, open-mindedness, open-handedness and trust, this place has become a much better place than it ever was then. Of that I can assure Synod.

With regard to the legislation, when we were in a minority there was no legislation and there were no Evangelical bishops. You do not need legislation to keep people out of appointments, the old boy network works jolly well. What you have here in this legislation is far better than we ever had as a minority, and besides that, legislation can be changed. I mean, we have done vacation of benefices, patronage, this, that and the perishing other, and put in codes of practice to make it more pastoral. We have a code of practice and this legislation: if we trust one another, surely it ought to work.

I was really sad to hear a colleague from St Albans, Sara Low, make the speech she did. I understand the fears but I think that some of her statements are unjustified – [*Several members:* No.] Bear with me, I did not interrupt any of you. Hugh referred to this as well, worrying about appointments and so on. This has been around ever since I can remember, and I fear I may have made similar statements when I was in a minority too, so I understand them; but again I think that this place, with the new formulas for Crown Appointments and other things that are going on, is much more open, trusting and real than it was then.

May I say to the Bishop of Sheffield, please, sir, do not fly away. Stay with us and pray. The Scriptures say that if my brother demands of me a coat I should give him my cloak. I offer you mine (*taking off his coat*), with my wallet in it, as an assurance that you can stay and work through this with us. Please vote for the Measure today.

The Bishop of Doncaster (Rt Revd Bill Persson): I appreciate what Philip has just been saying, but one of the things that needs to be noted is that the difference between being a minority in the past and being a minority now is the question of order. Before, you could be a minority and maybe live to fight another day, if 'fight' is not too awful a word, but if there is no longer a common order, that is almost impossible. I do not see how anyone who is a non-recogniser of women priests can, if this legislation goes through, in fact be a bishop and exercise his office properly. It is a question of order, and this needs to be said.

I want to speak briefly in response to one or two earlier Evangelical speakers who have told us how they have wrestled with this question and changed their mind. I have spent a great deal of time wrestling with the Scriptures myself and listening to and reflecting carefully on what others have said. I have been greatly blessed with much ecumenical experience and the pattern of order of others; I have received communion from a great many Free Church women ministers at different times, and I thank God for the ministry of our women deacons. Yet in my judgment the New Testament teaches with reasonable clarity that there is a pattern of God-given order in the life of the Church for the roles of men and women. It is not a role of dominance, of men over women, or false perceptions of authority or inequality of nature, although, as it happens, if we look at the sexual and marital disarray in society I wonder why we are so readily dismissive of a more traditional understanding of male/female relationships. [*Several members:* Oh!] Well, I know, it is very easy to protest, but it only goes to show how you are reflecting the fashion of the age when you respond like that.

It is not a matter of barriers or lines or circles. I believe in the wholeness of ministry. There is a glorious fulfilling ministry for any Christian, clergy or laity, men or women, and we should not focus so much on the ministry of the clergy that we forget the wholeness of the ministry of the laity; but I believe that in a God-given order within the Church it is not appropriate to have an ordained priesthood for women in the Church of England.

I do not want to get into the business of exchanging texts, I simply want to make the basic point that, while it is not exactly black and white in Scripture and while some will make more of the complexity than others, yet broadly in the interaction between Scripture and contemporary understanding the final judgment must be for one or the other, and I know on which side of that perception I believe it right to stand.

We do not want to be negative, whichever way the vote goes. It is very easy for those who have reservations to be terribly negative about whether it goes through, but it is equally dangerous to be negative if it does not go through. A friend of mine felt called by God to be a missionary in Burma: he was absolutely certain, he knew the country, it was God's call. He went to the missionary society concerned, was accepted and was waiting, and then suddenly Burma withdraw all visas and he did not go. God called him to Kenya. In fact, he was not called to Burma at all but to Kenya. God's 'no' for him was actually his 'yes'. Whichever way this goes, it will be 'no' for some of us - but is it not just possible that our 'no' may be God's 'yes'?

Revd Susan Hope (Sheffield): Any debate concerning the priesthood should, I think, be set firmly within the context from which it springs, namely the resurrection of Christ and the outpouring of the Holy Spirit, for the beginnings of the new order which is the Church are not biological but christological, and in baptism male and female become, through Jesus, partakers of the divine life. It is the sharing of the divine life which enables the Church to be a royal priesthood and to fulfil its calling to worship and to witness. Thus the Old Testament concept of the priesthood is both abolished and fulfilled in the priesthood of all believers, abolished as being of a separate holy group, fulfilled in total identification with the priesthood of Christ.

John Robinson has written that 'one of the revolutionary claims and characteristics of the early Church was what is called the common ownership – the *koinonia* – of Holy Spirit', and he continues, 'With the communalisation of the Holy Spirit went the communalisation of priesthood'. The implication of this communalisation of the priesthood is that priesthood is held in common in the Church, and that authority to forgive sins, to celebrate the Eucharist, to preach and teach the Gospel, is a communal authority held in the community by both men and women together, through the indwelling of the Holy Spirit. The priesthood of Christ is ours in the sense that it is held by the whole Body. It is a corporate priesthood rather than an individual one.

The priesthood of the individual ordained priest is of one piece with the communal priesthood, it is of the same fabric. It is we together, both male and female, who celebrate the Eucharist, we together who hold the authority to preach and proclaim the Gospel. The priest is one such as ourselves, called to represent and focus our common priesthood; the priest is icon of our common priesthood. When the community of male and female, clothed in the seamless robe of Christ's priesthood, act as the icon of Christ, taking bread, blessing, breaking, it is the individual priest who images the action of Christ in his Body, a Body made up of both male and female.

The coming of the Spirit on all flesh has meant too a communalisation of authority — 'sons and daughters will prophesy . . . Even on my servants, both men and women, I will pour out my Spirit in those days' — and that authority is held by us in common in the Body, a Body of male and female. It is only vested in an individual as representative of a commonly held authority, authority already given, which men and women hold together. Thus the authority of leadership is a focus, an expression, of the authority of the Body.

The debate, therefore, is not properly a debate about whether women can become priestly or can have authority, for the seamless robe of Christ's priesthood has been flung over the whole Body. The debate is properly about whether the Church in our generation believes the social and cultural restraints which have so far inhibited women from acting as a focus for our common priesthood to have been lifted. I believe, along with many others, that those restraints have been lifted. This is not the importation of secular feminism, it is the making explicit of what is implicit in the Pauline gospel of the Church. It is an outward expression of that inward and glorious reality, that the priesthood is given not to one but to all, because all share together in the one and only priesthood of Christ.

The Archdeacon of Macclesfield (Ven. John Gaisford): We have concentrated so far, and rightly, on the cost to the Church in terms of ministry and mission, were this legislation to be successful; we have not yet considered the cost to the Church, in parish and in diocese, the cost in financial terms, were the Measure to be passed. We know that money must never dictate matters in the life of the Church, but we would be short-sighted indeed were we to ignore the financial consequences altogether. Financial consequences there must be because, even were the Measure to be passed, it could not come into operation unless the Financial Provisions Measure were also accepted. I have no intention of discussing this now but we must accept the implications contained in it when we vote this afternoon. The cost will be great, as spelt out in the Miscellaneous Paper that we have all received. No matter how conservative any estimate regarding the number of those leaving the Church or at what stage in their ministry, we know that such resignations will affect very seriously the amount of money available from the Church Commissioners towards allocation for stipends. We are told that for every hundred such resignations it will mean a reduction of £1 million per annum, and the cost will be higher if those who resign are in their fifties because compensation will be payable until the age of 60.

Figures can be bandied about and they have been on all sides. Estimates of those who might leave, were this legislation to be passed, range from 50 to 3,000; but let us be certain that, no matter how small or large the financial cost may be, the money will have to be found in the parishes – and we are already in serious difficulties, with reductions taking place at the moment and envisaged over the next two years at least.

This Measure will be disastrous pastorally and theologically. It will also be disastrous in its financial implications, and I hope that the Synod will take this into account when it comes to vote.

The Bishop of Southwark (Rt Revd Roy Williamson): I am trying to obey the advice given by the President this morning not to repeat points that have already been made in the debate. As far as I am aware, this particular point has not been made, at least in an Irish accent.

Throughout the history of the Church of God there seem to have been two dominating and recurring attitudes in the Church. There were those who were concerned for survival, safety, solidarity, tradition, all of which are of course important, and there were those who were concerned about risk, openness and vulnerability, and these things too are important. Both views are clearly held in this Synod, and, if I am honest, I will admit that there is a bit of both of them in me. At the end of the day, however, I find myself compelled towards the second view. Some words of John Robinson of blessed memory, who ministered in my present diocese and whose grave lies in my former diocese, words of his spoken in a different context, have burnt themselves into my mind when considering the issue before us. Just as the New Testament bids us have as high a doctrine of the ministry as we like, as long as our doctrine of the Church is higher, so it commands us to have as high a doctrine of the Church as we may, provided our doctrine of the Kingdom is higher. As far as in me lies I am trying to seek first the Kingdom of God.

One of the marks or characteristics of that Kingdom is justice. I found myself in my former diocese and now in my present diocese, like many others in the Synod this afternoon, having to stand up and be counted by confronting in the name of God some of the chronic injustices of our society and finding myself at risk, exposed and vulnerable, with some of the cruellest criticism coming from members of the Church; but in the cause of justice I could do none other, which is why I shall vote for this motion this afternoon. At the end of the day, having tried to balance all the nuances of the theological and ecclesiological arguments on both sides, I am compelled by what I perceive to be the cause of justice.

My brothers and sisters, I genuinely and completely respect the views of others in this Synod and I speak only for myself when I say that I cannot with any degree of integrity challenge the injustices of society and turn a blind eye to the apparent injustice within the Church which prevents women from testing their vocation to the priesthood.

Throughout my life, since I have come to England, I have been on the receiving end of Irish jokes. (Only the English are stupid enough to laugh at them.) Yet while we have been struggling — and various reasons have been given why we are struggling; my own conviction is that we have this treasure in earthen vessels and that is why: we are struggling with our own 'clayness' — the dear old Church of Ireland that is supposed to be fifty years behind the times has crept up and got on with the job. (*Applause*) I hope that Synod will realise that though I periodically use humour it is never for humour's sake, there is always a serious point behind it. It seems to me that if the Church of Ireland has got on with the job as has the Anglican Church in South Africa, in two lands where people's lives are being shattered by violence day after day, it may very well be that in those kinds of circumstance they get even a thing like this into perspective.

Of all the arguments opposing the ordination of women to the priesthood, and as one who was called to maintain the unity of the Church, I feel the weight of the sincerely held conviction of many that because of the threat to the unity of the Church the time may not yet be right; but as a seeker first of the Kingdom, I feel that if there is injustice to be removed the only time to do it is now. It is a risk I am prepared to take, casting myself on the mercy of God which, when you think of it, is something we all have to do at the end of the day and at the end of time.

Revd John Broadhurst (London): The last speech was a very powerful one, but I must say to the Bishop that justice is only done if we give what God wants given, and it is that question which we must grapple with and not our contemporary views of what may or may not be just.

I want to talk about how we make change. Because much of what I wanted to say has already been said, I have thrown away my original speech. When you, Your Grace, introduced the debate you asked how we make our decisions and you drew attention to St Peter and his resistance to God's will with regard to evangelisation of the Gentiles. You pointed out how St Peter had a vision and that St Peter was wrong in the views that he held. St Peter lost the case, but St Peter was not wrong because he had a vision, he was wrong because the view he held was contrary to Our Lord's expressed words, and he was wrong because the view that he held was contrary to the later development of Judaism, to the universal salvation centred on Jerusalem, to the vision at the end of Malachi of all nations worshipping God. St Peter was completely out of touch and it was not the vision that made him wrong but rather the fact that he was defying the redemption of the nations. Universal redemption was a picture springing out of Judaism.

The present legislation is not right because we have had a vision or wrong because we have failed to have one, it is wrong because it is at variance with the Jewish and Christian tradition that we have inherited. It is that point which challenges us. Scripture, tradition, the universal tradition of the Church, two thousand years, no, more, four, five, six thousand years of history. Judaism was unique in its vision that its religious leadership was male. It is that rock from which we are hewn and it is that rock that we must be faithful to, our Jewish/Christian tradition. That same tradition is against today's legislation.

This morning Dr Avis told a very amusing story about the children in his school being asked why the Church only ordained men. The children saw the point and understood the tradition: because Jesus chose only men, we choose only men. Dr Avis went on to ask his children 'What now?' and the children gave the contemporary view, that now it would be half and half. But the children do not understand what we understand or rather what we should understand. [*Several members:* Oh!] No, what we should understand, for Jesus was God's disclosure of himself for all time, for all nations, for all people. To say that Jesus was socially and culturally conditioned on essential matters is to make him less than God's disclosure.

More than that, Jesus's view of women was at variance with that of the age in which he lived. Jesus was a social revolutionary on this subject, and yet he did not choose women apostles, although he did choose a woman to be the first witness of the Resurrection. Wrestle with it: that is the tradition that we are to preserve, that is the tradition which is valuable for us. Jesus chose male leaders. We may understand it, we may not; we may find it easy to live with, we may find it difficult; but it is the fact of the Gospel, hard for some.

What he did is normative for us. It is very easy to look at things and misunderstand them. We heard some very emotional stories this morning about a line across the floor of Durham Cathedral. Durham Cathedral was a monastery. I have found myself excluded from parts of convents because I am male.

I want to reiterate what several bishops have said: the legislation affects anybody who holds the traditional view, and anybody who believes what the

Church has consistently taught for two thousand years will be excluded, whatever the assurances we are given, excluded by his own convictions, for if I am to sit in unimpaired communion with this Church if it ordains women I can only do so by fatally compromising my own deeply held convictions. I do not say that easily, I find it hard because I passionately love this Church which I have served for the best part of thirty years; but my convictions are God-given, and I cannot compromise them, for if I do I risk my soul.

The Bishop of Durham (Rt Revd David Jenkins): — Bishop of Durham, 2 — no, 4, 4 — I always count the Archbishops as being beyond number and quantity! I have done it before, have I not? So I wonder, Your Grace, No. 1, as No. 4, if we have reached the point in this Synod, as we come near to the vote, where we have to stop being balanced in our attempts to understand and argue with one another. Ought we not perhaps rather to be broken by the shame we are bringing on God, his Christ and the Gospel? Is it not shameful to be quarrelling as we are about women in the Church when the whole world is torn by poverty, strife and lostness, and to be doing it in the full glare of the media?

Is it not disgraceful that we have so little faith in the catholicity of Christ's incarnation for all and in the catholicity of the sacrament of his body and blood that we confine that sacrament to men's hands? Surely women's hands are as human and as able to be hallowed by God's grace and calling?

Should we not perhaps feel ashamed and angry that we talk blandly about pain on both sides and we are advised not to be angry about whatever comes from this vote? For a No vote condemns us to five more years of wasted energy, and consigns called, tested and trusted women in our diaconate and elsewhere to more years of condescension and, I do honestly fear, oppression. How can we not be angry?

Yet I know — and I mean that, I know — in the fabric of my being that the persons in my diocese who oppose this legislation include priests who I am sure are devoted and disciplined priests with whom I personally share a zeal for the Gospel and for Christ's sacraments. They will be angry if this legislation is passed.

How are we to respond to all this? It brings me near to despair when our Church so obscures the glories of the Gospel at such a time of need and opportunity. It nearly breaks my heart, for I have been long enough in my diocese to care that my women deacons should be freed for their priestly calling and not be left in distress, and also to care that my opposing brethren should not be separated and put into distress.

Do we not have to realise that to be near to despair and to be threatened with a broken heart is to be very near where Christ has been before, and so to understand that there can still be saving grace if we seek to live together by forgiveness? We have to choose: to follow the majority in becoming free to ordain women to the priesthood, or to be blocked for the time being by the minority. Can we not throw ourselves on the mercy of God by choosing to go ahead in humility, confusion, distress and togetherness? Not of course beyond all reasonable doubt, for who is ever there? but together in reasonable hope and faith. With the complexities of our two-thirds voting system in three different Houses, the result of our vote will in any case be something like a statistical chance. We shall achieve not the will of God but the opportunity to find out where he wills to take us, whatever the outcome.

Is it not Anglican to leave theological loose ends and questions yet to be answered? The accompanying legislation that we have is, I am sure, flawed, but it has been offered for honourable and Anglican reasons. We know that we must choose to ordain or not to ordain, but we refuse to choose to exclude disagreeing brothers and sisters. We are not trying to square an impossible circle but to live openly to one another by the possibilities of God's enabling grace.

I hope, therefore, that we will muster the necessary majorities to go ahead with this legislation, but surely we may all be free to vote faithfully in all humility as we judge we must. This is because we know that, whatever the result of the vote, we have not yet got the will of God. We shall only have the opportunity together to go on seeking his will, receiving his grace and offering him service.

Surely, brothers and sisters in Christ, it cannot be that our vote will destroy the being, worship and service of the Church. It cannot be so simply because of forgiveness: God will enable and renew. It cannot be so because of simple catholicity: God will continue his universal purposes and honour his universal sacraments. It cannot be so simply because God has called us: we must vote as we must, and then we must continue together, in humility, in hope and in the forgiving and empowering grace of God.

The Chairman: After the next two speakers I hope that we may be able to wind up the debate. If there are still members standing then, I will impose a three-minute speech limit.

Mr Michael Hughes (Salisbury): I have talked against this for a long time and I want to tell Synod honestly that I now do not know which way to vote. The reasons in favour are obvious: many women would make good priests, and it seems sexist and unjust to deny them that. The reasons against are that there is nothing in the Bible, nothing in revelation, no consensus among Christians. There is a great majority in our Church in favour of it but we know, from the faithful with the golden calf or when they shouted for Barabbas, that the majority can be wrong, so we cannot always go with the majority. I have looked at these two things and, on balance, I have decided to speak against this in the past; but now I know that my reason is not good enough because we are the Church, and the reason why a minority Middle Eastern sect is now the biggest and still growing Church in the world is because God gives truth to his Church. My reasoning does not matter; what matters is that through prayer I ought to know the will of God – and, before God, I do not.

We have had a lot of letters – you have probably had more than me, Your Grace –from both sides, and they were not from freaks but from good Christian people, passionately concerned about this. I wish we had had one-tenth as many letters when we talked about making young people into Christians. Many of them have said that if it does not go their way they will leave the Church. Many of them have said that they will cancel their covenant; not many of them have said that they will increase their covenant if it goes their way! I have talked to those outside the Church, those in the universities, and most outside the Church have been in favour of the motion because they say that the Church must conform on sexual equality; but no-one has suggested that if we do ordain women priests they might then be tempted to explore the Gospel, and that is a sad thing.

The letters show the damage we have done by bringing this without consensus. Either way we lose priests, it costs a lot of money, we have members sadly turning away, either because the Church is perceived as faithless or because it is perceived as non-credible. Whichever way I vote I will be responsible for hurt and damage to the faith of thousands like the writers of those letters. How can anyone after this vote, whichever way it goes, want to go and do a dance of joy? There is no joy, only shame for this Synod as we reach what we have brought the Church to.

After the vote, whichever side wins, if there is any winning, we must ensure four things. We must not bring this back here for years; if we do not start looking outwards now this Church will die and deserve to die. We must stop using deacons as priests with a couple of missing sentences, which erodes the whole understanding of what the priesthood is. We must increase the time and talents that we give to the Church to more than make up for the shortfall of those who are unable to go on. We must work to comfort and sustain all those who are damaged.

In conclusion, I do not know. I have not been given the wisdom, and I probably shall not be before the vote; but I have been called to vote on this matter for the Church and it is not for me to abstain. If I cannot see God's will by the vote then I will, sadly, vote against, believing that we cannot change the Church in this fundamental way unless we are sure that it is God's will. How fortunate are they who know God's will on this, for that is all that matters: may God's will be done.

Canon John Stanley (Liverpool): I am not John Gladwin, Provost of Sheffield – The Thunderer got it wrong – I am John Stanley, Vicar of Huyton.

I have deliberately waited until towards the end of this debate because I believe that what is going to happen in the next half-hour may well be for the Church of England a watershed, whatever the result of the voting. I do not know which way the vote will go; every indication is that it will be a very narrow vote, one way or the other. My inclination is to believe that it is better that it should pass with a narrow majority than fail with a narrow majority.

The Bishop of Durham expressed far more eloquently the things that were in my mind to say at this particular point than I can. Perhaps if I may add just a sentence to what he said: if all the energy that went into the many letters that we all received – they ran into their hundreds – will go after this vote towards the healing that must take place in our Church, I believe that whichever way the vote goes we shall be making a positive move in the right direction.

No-one has said yet – and I do not quite know how to say this – that if this Measure should fail, we need to say to the women deacons: the vast majority of the Church are behind you in wanting to test your vocation to the priesthood and you do not belong to a narrow minority in the Church, for the majority are behind you. It will be small consolation but it ought to be some consolation if the vote goes in that direction.

After a very long time of trying to see what Scripture has taught and teaches, and what we must do on this issue today, I have at long last been able to get my own thinking together, and I shall walk through the Aye doors (with the little green man above them).

It is difficult to know what the future holds for us as a Church, and I know that many are saying – and their voices have been heard here today – 'We have not quite got it right yet, wait.' I am reminded of the old lady who, when decimal currency was introduced, said that she was not against decimal currency but she would rather it was introduced when all the old people had died. I have a feeling that if we wait we will go on waiting. Therefore I would urge the Synod to go through the Aye doors. (*Calls for a vote*)

The Chairman imposed a speech limit of three minutes.

Mrs Katherine Heidt (Gloucester): I think we must go back just one more time to the legislation and we must be quite clear that if we pass it we will be acting in a most irresponsible and negative manner. Is it not irresponsible and negative to enshrine in law a dual Church? How can we in all conscience, no matter how we feel about the principle, do such a thing? This is legislation for schism because, for the first time in the history of the Church of England, there would be doubt about the validity of the orders of the priests who would be celebrating at our altars. We would be divided one from another at the very heart of our communion, at the Eucharist itself. A Church built on a breach of communion cannot flourish, can have no mission and can certainly have no Good News.

I have some first-hand experience of this in America where I have likened it to a civil war situation with even families divided against each other. If this were not the case, then there would be no Episcopal Synod of America and no continuing Churches. If it does not work in such a large land mass, how can it possibly work on an island? (*Some dissent*) It is true. People have said, 'We are already divided, so let's get on with it.' Let us rather try to heal our divisions, to do as the Lord has asked, that they all may be one, and not legislate ourselves into an institutionalised disunity. I urge members to vote against this legislation. (*More calls for a vote*)

The Chairman: As President, I invite you all to co-operate in moving towards the closure, but of course you have the right to stand. However, I invite you to consider if you still have arguments to add to the debate which have not been considered.

Mrs Marie Howell (London): The Bible tells us that God created men and women in his own image and likeness. When God told us that he created us in his own image, he did not mean that our physical appearance was like his, he meant our souls, our minds, our capacity for reason and compassion, love and friendship. These are the aspects of humanity that are in his image. Surely this belies the argument that only men can be the true representatives of Christ as priest. At the time of Christ's coming, society was structured in a patriarchal fashion, men dominant and women subservient. In such a time it would have served no useful purpose to choose women as apostles as, for the most part, they had no voice even within their own home – so how could they spread the word of God? Even so, Jesus did not ignore them; it was to the three Marys that he appeared after the Resurrection. He praised their work and condemned those who would denigrate them, as in the incident with Mary Magdalene.

Which one of us can say without a doubt that if Our Saviour came on earth today he would choose men rather than women, that he would deny them the opportunity to go out and do his work? Women's talents are God-given. Why should we deny them the opportunity to do God's work if they have received God's call into the priesthood? Why should we as members of Christ's Church forbid them the right to go about his work? It is time for us to move forward at the end of the 20th century and allow women to fulfil their roles as equal partners in Christ.

Rather than get involved in theological arguments, already widely dealt with, I would like to focus on three points. Some people say that if the legislation for women to the priesthood goes through it will affect our chances for unity with the Romans, but I do not think so because they are not in communion with us and they do not recognise us. Because it will not go away, we must vote yes and move on to reconciliation and growth. I am concerned for the credibility of the Church since the Synod stated in 1975 that there is no theological objection to the ordination of women. As a Church we are already divided. Some people are saying that we would separate them from the Church that they know and love. What about the hurt to women who are denied the right to use pastorally and spiritually the full gifts that God has given them? Do you think that they are not suffering too? The full range of women's talents has been neglected for far too long. We must not minimise the hurt and anger of the majority of our Church if this Measure is defeated. The passage of Scripture that inspires me is, 'You did not choose me, I chose you.' (*The Chairman rang the bell.*) (*More calls for a vote*)

Revd Roger Arguile (Lichfield): I am sorry to take up yet more time of the Synod because I know that members are impatient to get on with the business. In the Tiller Report which I read and which I dislike, a managerial concept of priesthood is advanced, but in about the fourth page of the report it is pointed out that the reason for its argument is partly the shortage of male clergy. It says, though it disagrees with its conclusion, that numerically the problem would disappear if women were ordained, the problem that Tiller sought to address. I have written to everybody who has written to me about the issue, saying that, apart from the other arguments that have been rehearsed, the Church is starving through lack of priests. I see, as the Sheffield quota goes down and down for my diocese each year and parishes are amalgamated, how desperate the situation is becoming. I want to see women priests for a lot of reasons, but one of them is because I want to see Weston and Gayton and Fradswell and Hixon and Milwich and Stowe-by-Chartley and so on have priests, and they do not have them at the moment.

The Chairman: I see no-one standing! (*Laughter and applause*) I want to thank Synod for the tone and standard of this debate. We have listened to one another.

The Archdeacon of Leicester: I hope not to detain the Synod, it has been a long and wearisome day and we may yet have other things to do. Most of us have appointments later on today!

I hope that the Synod will forgive me — there have been so many speeches that it is almost impossible to pick out all the individuals and points that need to be addressed in the closing speech, and I must gather various things together. There has been a considerable overlap in the speeches and in many cases speakers have answered one another, and I would not want to add to what has been said by some. There have been two notable maiden speeches for which we are very grateful, the first from the Revd Penny Martin and the other from Sara Low; they have been valuable contributions to the debate. There has also been another valuable contribution to the debate from whatever may be termed the opposite of a maiden speaker, the Bishop of Doncaster. He made a noble speech. We shall miss his wisdom and thoughtfulness in the Synod. There will be an opportunity to thank him for what he has contributed to the central affairs of the Church of England later this week, but just for now I want to put on record how much we owe him. (*Applause*)

Two speakers this afternoon made a number of points in their speeches, and it is probably better if I address myself to them first before I move to the more gathered approach. The first was the Archbishop of York who was characteristically lucid and concise and who, with that deceptively leisurely air of his, managed to put three punches into five minutes when it would have taken most people nearly half an hour to do it. First, he referred back to the Bishop of Sheffield who was unconvinced by the good intentions of the proponents of the legislation and asked how on earth we would work it. The Archbishop said that the legislation provides for us to go on together, but that is the problem and precisely my point: the legislation does not provide for us to go on together. The Archbishop said that faith was impoverished if we exclude minorities – I think that is the word he used. You see, the problem is that we cannot go on together if we actually build into this legislation a bias which in the end will ease out one particular point of view. Make no mistake about it, this legislation has that bias; it does not provide for people to go on together for an unlimited time, it builds in obsolescence.

Second, the Archbishop said that we should not be afraid of differences. Well, you could say that in a Church which held together pluralism of belief within a common order, but for the first time we shall enshrine in the law of the Church, fossilise in the law of the Church, institutionalise in the law of the Church a failure to provide a commonly accepted ministry. We are actually building in the provision that a parish can withhold its assent from the authenticity of a minister. You can live with certain differences but I do not think that you can live with that.

Third, the Archbishop referred to what he called the conspiracy theory. We all know perfectly well that most of us have some form of a conspiracy theory at some time in our lives, but look round and ask how many senior appointments have been made in dioceses – I am not talking about the episcopate now, I am talking about posts like archdeacons and so on – from among opponents of the legislation. I tell you this: since this legislation has been running round the country, one-third of those particular posts have not gone to people who are opposed to the legislation. Mr Lovegrove referred to the old boy network, and the old boy network of course has two sides; but the fact is that the network provides for most of the appointments and therefore you will continue to multiply a particular point of view.

The other speaker I want to say a little more to than just generally is Professor McClean. He actually criticised Mr Craig and the Bishop of London for having recourse to an earlier document in this exercise, GS 764, I think, but he must recall that it was in GS 764, which is still there on the record and has never been withdrawn, that the House of Bishops set out the principles on which the legislation should be based. It was the then Archbishop of Canterbury who said 'The House [of Bishops] believes that, if the Synod wishes to ordain women to the priesthood, this is the way it has to be done.' The Synod asked for legislation in accordance with the Bishops' guidelines in GS 764, and in July 1988 Professor McClean assured the Synod that those guidelines had been faithfully followed. The Bishop of Sheffield, Mr Craig and the Bishop of London all referred back to that and, I believe, did so justifiably.

Professor McClean also spoke of the provision for bishops who are opposed to the legislation. There is still space for such bishops, he said, but the fact is that there is only space if they are not going to try to act like bishops, as I made clear in my opening speech.

When I began I set out six objections which, I said, the proponents of the legislation must answer if they were to convince the opponents that the legislation was not what it appeared to be. The first was that the legislation proposes irreversible action arising from a theology which cannot be demonstrated beyond all doubt to be required by Scripture as understood by the Church through the ages. There has been a good deal of to-ing and fro-ing about this headship argument in the course of the debate, and some of it was before lunch and maybe behind a kind of closed curtain in the minds of some of us, but I remind the Synod that towards the end of the morning the Bishop of Newcastle actually took a firm line with us – and he is chairman of the Doctrine Commission, which is not always noted for a firm line in various matters. With characteristic clarity and fairness he chided the Bishop of Guildford and said very clearly that it was misleading to enlist tradition in favour of the legislation, that to describe the legislation as consonant with Scripture was a disputed thing and that since the matter was uncertain it was quite wrong to base legislation on it. After lunch, the Bishop of Sheffield told us that the authority of Scripture would be fatally weakened by this proposal.

I expect that most of us feel, when we hear a debate about a thing like headship or other arguments of that kind, just a little as though we are watching a ping-pong match and losing track sometimes of who has the ball. In an attempt to make sense of it, I think that what I have most firmly remaining in my mind is a picture of Sir Norman Anderson, the great Evangelical chairman of the House of Laity, standing in the place now occupied with such distinction by Professor McClean – I see that it is empty at the moment but it usually has him in it, because he is a faithful member of the Synod. Norman Anderson listened to a debate such as we have had today, discussing disputed biblical evidence, and at the end he said to the Synod – and his words are imprinted on my memory – 'in the end I come face to face with the plain meaning of Scripture'.

I hear what is said about the headship issue and I try to follow the debate, but in the end I come face to face with the plain meaning of Scripture, and I cannot believe that God would have left its intent so obscure as to need all the fine points made in this debate to make it clear to me.

Moving to my second point, I said that the trouble with this legislation was that it proposed action in a primary matter of faith and order by an authority which was claimed without the precedent of Scripture or the authority of the Church. That has been contested, and contested by some who have confused what I meant by talking about unity with Rome. I am not talking about proposed unity with Rome, or about taking a cue from the Vatican; I am talking about the faith and order that we claim to share with other great historic Churches, and it is that abdication of our commitment that I deplore in the legislation.

My third point which was about the episcopate and the presbyterate was unchallenged. As for the rest, it is really a matter for the Synod to decide whether it is the legislation that it is prepared to support.

Something has been said about justice and something has been said about the view outside this House, but in the end this is about faithfulness to the tradition and to the faith. To support the motion inflicts on the Church of England this legislation and the polity of congregationalism that it enshrines, without hope of withdrawal. To reject the legislation, because it is inappropriate, unfair, irreversible, by voting No is an affirmation of Anglican inclusiveness, an affirmation of the continued search for consensus, an affirmation of what the Dean of St Paul's called a more excellent way. If we vote No, our vote is actually to affirm the full assurance of faith and the maintenance of the authority of Scripture and apostolic order; it is a vote for the integrity and mission of the Church of England which, put simply in Our Lord's words, is about his last recorded prayer, that the Church may be one that the world may believe.

The Bishop of Guildford, in reply: I think it was at a corresponding point in a previous debate on the ordination of women that Oswald Clark responded by saying, 'I will not keep you long, as Henry VIII said to his wives.' Having quoted Oswald Clark in that sense, I hope Synod will understand if I do not quote him further.

It is not possible to respond to all the points that have been made in a debate which has been spirited but generous in its style, but there are some points which I must try to attend to and I apologise if inevitably there are many other points which I cannot deal with in detail.

The question was raised, particularly this morning, of whether we have authority to take this step. Those who argue that we should make such a decision only when we have the agreement of Catholic and Eastern Christendom have to come to terms with our membership of the Anglican Communion. A growing number of Anglican provinces are taking this step and if the Church of England says that it cannot take this decision without the agreement of Rome and the East, we are putting ourselves increasingly out of relationship with our fellow Anglicans in the hope of closer relations with Rome and the East. That seems to me to be hazardous.

We of course have to take seriously our membership of the whole Western Catholic tradition, but we live and work in the tradition of our own Church of England which has recognised ever since the Reformation that at times it is necessary to accept responsibility for our own decisions in the pursuit of truth. We did that, for instance, when we brought laity into partnership with clergy and bishops in the determination of doctrine, and that new role for laity formalised in synodical government has distanced us in some measure from the Eastern Churches and from Rome; but we effected that development without formalised consultation with those Churches because of our conviction that it was a return to a better ecclesiology. So I think that we just have to accept the fact that on occasion we must take responsibility for our own decisions and, having made such a decision, to offer what we do as a contribution to Christendom.

Then there is the matter of tradition. The Bishop of Newcastle tried hard to pull the carpet from under my feet this morning: perhaps I may adopt the metaphor used by Newman, who accused Pusey of discharging an olive branch from a catapult. I did indeed make a high claim that this development is required of us by tradition. Of course I recognise that the Bishop of Newcastle (who up to now has been a friend of mine) is free to challenge that; what I was doing was saying quite firmly that it is not that we think that this development is not against Scripture and tradition; as we perceive it, this is actually required of us as we look again at Scripture and tradition. I will continue the debate with him afterwards, but I am not prepared to withdraw what I boldly stated as the view of those who argue for the legislation.

The Bishop of Sheffield — I am sorry to be taking issue with my colleagues and I have to recognise that the diocese of Guildford and the diocese of Sheffield are linked (or were) — challenged us as to whether those of us who were proponents of the legislation actually believed in a concrete reality of revelation. Those were his words. I am surprised at the word 'concrete' because I believe that tradition is a living and organic truth, grounded in Scripture as the Spirit of God leads us to put old truth into new terms. Every time a bishop licenses or institutes a priest he repeats those words, that we believe in the faith which we are called upon to proclaim afresh in each generation, not 'again' but 'afresh'; and what is required of us is that we should restate tradition in order to preserve it. I repeat what I said this morning: the ordination of women to the priesthood may be contrary to tradition in the sense that it has not happened before, but it is not contrary to tradition in the sense of truth as it has been handed down to us. If I may throw a counter-challenge to the Bishop of Newcastle, I have to say that I note that he did not engage with the arguments that I put forward on the basis of our understanding of the Incarnation.

I want to turn also to the matter of generosity, the generosity of the legislation and generosity of spirit, because we have work to do here. The legislation, it seems to me, is pastoral in its understanding and intention, but there will inevitably be work to do in order to ensure that the Church of England remains both Catholic and Reformed. We cannot assume that that will happen without all working together. I also want to say that at the end of the day I for one, and I am sure the rest of us, believe in a God of resurrection. I believe that God takes our fragmented lives, our divided Church and our broken world and uses them as the raw material out of which to create his new life. I do not therefore think that we have to wait until everything is proved beyond reasonable doubt, because we believe in a God of resurrection.

We have heard today arguments about the ordination of women curiously similar to those rehearsed in 1959 when the proposal was to allow women into lay Readership, the ministry of the Word. It was argued thirty-odd years ago that such a step departed from the age-old tradition of the Church, that it would hinder reunion, that there was insufficient evidence in the New Testament to justify it and that it was a matter for the whole Church. A generation later, women are accepted as Readers and they have enriched our ministry of the Word – and the arguments and anxieties of a generation ago seem exaggerated. If now we take a step towards women in the priesthood, in thirty years' time our arguments of today may well appear exaggerated, just as I guess that there are many people on the edge of the life of the Church who may well think that today we are making heavy weather of this issue and, as they would put it, they 'can't quite see what all the fuss is about'.

We have to make a decision. The decision concerns the relationship between men and women, and so it touches deep emotions in all of us. The decision derives from our understanding of God, and so we argue with spiritual passion. The decision affects the nature, style and extent of the Church of England which for many of us is part of the fabric of our being, so it is no surprise that there are strong passions and emotions around. In all that, whichever way the vote goes, we must work to keep the Church of England open, open to people of differing views, open to people still searching for the truth, open to the continuing guidance of God. Now, however, we face an historic opportunity for the Church of England to move forward in accordance with scriptural truth and with tradition. If we do not vote this matter through today, it will not melt away. We are all realistic enough to know that it will be back in a few years' time and that we shall have much the same wrestling match again. So I put it squarely to the Synod that, having worked through the arguments, having hammered out the details of the legislation, surely it is better to grasp the issue and the opportunity now. Do not let us procrastinate. Having reached this point, let us get on with it.

We need to make this decision not on a wave of emotion, though this is undoubtedly an emotive occasion, not even, I dare to say, out of compassion for women who yearn to test their vocation, though those people are never far from our minds, but on the grounds of Scripture, tradition and cool reasoning. A majority of our Church is waiting for us to make this decision. So I ask the Synod to take a step forward into the future, God's future, confident that he will lead us into this truth. I ask the Synod to vote firmly, clearly and confidently for this legislation.

The Chairman: In Synod's name I want to thank the two main speakers, the Archdeacon of Leicester and the Bishop of Guildford. (*Applause*)

Will you please stand? Before we vote, we stand in silence for private reflection and prayer as together, as a Synod, we seek God's will. (*A prayer was said by The Chairman, followed by the giving of the Peace.*)

The motion was put and The Chairman, pursuant to SO 48(d)(iii), ordered a division by Houses, with the following result:

	Ayes	Noes
House of Bishops	39	13
House of Clergy	176	74
House of Laity	169	82

The motion was therefore carried.

The Chairman: The Measure now stands committed to the Legislative Committee.

THE CHAIR

The Archbishop of York *took the Chair at 5.00 p.m.*

The Chairman: I declare on behalf of both the Presidents, the Prolocutors and the Chairman and Vice-Chairman of the House of Laity that the requirements of Article 7 and Article 8 of the Constitution have been complied with in respect of this item of business.

Professor David McClean: I beg to move:

'That Canon C4 B (Of Women Priests) be finally approved.'

This draft Canon is the means by which the General Synod exercises the power conferred by clause 1 of the Measure which we have just approved.

The Chairman: Is there any debate? (*No response*)

The motion was put and The Chairman, pursuant to SO 48(d)(iii), ordered a division by Houses, with the following result:

	Ayes	Noes
House of Bishops	35	8
House of Clergy	164	61
House of Laity	160	69

The motion was therefore carried.

Professor David McClean: I beg to move:

'That the Canon entitled "Amending Canon No 13" be finally approved.'

This draft Amending Canon contains a miscellaneous series of amendments to existing Canons consequential upon or related to the decisions that we have taken this afternoon. Paragraphs 1 and 2 are directly consequential on the terms of the main Measure; paragraphs 3 and 4 spell out the effects in particular contexts of cathedral or parish resolutions; and paragraph 5 makes it easier for an archdeacon to appoint another minister to carry out an induction on his behalf.

The Chairman: I declare on behalf of both the Presidents, the Prolocutors and the Chairman and Vice-Chairman of the House of Laity that the requirements of Article 7 and Article 8 of the Constitution have been complied with in respect of this item of business.

Is there any debate? (*No response*)

The motion was put and The Chairman, pursuant to SO 48(iii)(d), *ordered a division by Houses, with the following result:*

	Ayes	Noes
House of Bishops	40	5
House of Clergy	175	50
House of Laity	168	72

The motion was therefore carried.

Professor David McClean: I beg to move:

'That the Petition for Her Majesty's Royal Assent and Licence (GS 832D) be adopted.'

Before a Canon is promulged and executed it is necessary to obtain Her Majesty's Royal Assent and Licence, and this is sought in the petition, the text of which is before the Synod. The petition will of course only be presented when the Measure itself receives the Royal Assent, but it is our custom to approve the text at this stage.

The Chairman: Is there any debate? I see no-one standing with intent! This does not require a division by Houses.

The motion was put and carried.

Professor David McClean: I beg to move:

'That the Measure entitled "Ordination of Women (Financial Provisions) Measure" be finally approved.'

Clause 12 of the main Measure provides that it cannot come into force unless the Synod makes provision for the relief of hardship incurred by persons resigning from ecclesiastical service by reason of opposition to the promulgation of Canon C4 B. This Financial Provisions Measure is in that way tied into the main Measure. It has always been a part of the same package of proposals, and it appears as a separate Measure only because it was thought at one time that the two might move at different speeds through the synodical process.

Members of Synod will have received the steering committee's report bringing up to date the material that we supplied at an earlier stage about the financial implications. I am sorry that the report was circulated with the pages printed in some disarray. I think it is fair to say that there is nothing in the new report which introduces factors which have not been already fully discussed by the Synod. It has been a long day, and I move without further ado.

The Chairman: The motion is now open for debate, and I see no-one wishing to speak.

The motion was put and The Chairman, pursuant to SO 48(d)(iii), ordered a division by Houses, with the following result:

	Ayes	Noes
House of Bishops	35	0
House of Clergy	225	7
House of Laity	220	11

The motion was therefore carried.

The Chairman: The Measure now stands committed to the Legislative Committee.

Under SO 42 I move:

'That the Synod do now adjourn until 10.00 a.m. on Thursday 12 November.' (*Applause*)

I take it that the applause signifies assent.

The Session was adjourned at 5.55 p.m.

ABBREVIATIONS

Adn	Archdeacon	Dn	Deacon
Abp	Archbishop	Dn-in-c	Deacon-in-charge
ACC	Anglican Consultative Council	Dss	Deaconess
ACCM	Advisory Council for the Church's Ministry	educ	educated
		EIG	Ecclesiastical Insurance Group
Asst	Assistant	Hosp	Hospital
b	born	P-in-c	Priest-in-charge
BCC	British Council of Churches	Preb	Prebendary
BM	Board of Mission	R	Rector
BMU	Board for Mission and Unity	RD	Rural Dean
Bp	Bishop	Relig	Religious
Bps	Bishops, Bishop's, Bishops'	RSCM	Royal School of Church Music
BSR	Board for Social Responsibility	Rtd	Retired
C	Curate	Sch	School
Cathl	Cathedral	Sec	Secretary
CCBI	Council of Churches for Britain and Ireland	Soc	Society
		Th Coll	Theological College
CCC	Council for the Care of Churches	TR	Team Rector
CCU	Council for Christian Unity	TV	Team Vicar, Television
Coll	College	Univ	University
Commn	Commission	V	Vicar
CRPOF	Committee for Relations with People of Other Faiths	w	with
		WAOW	Women Against the Ordination of Women
CTE	Churches Together in England		
Ctee	Committee	WCC	World Council of Churches
DBF	Diocesan Board of Finance		

Th Coll Bristol   **am**, MA, LLB

c Humphrey Perkins Sch Barrow-on-Soar; King's Coll
le Coll Oxford; St Stephen's House Th Coll; Ripon Hall
6; TV St Chad Blakenall Heath 1976-83; TV St Bertelin
of Clergy Diocesan Synod

mar Sch Bristol;

    D, PHD

v; Teacher with   r George Monoux Grammar Sch; London Univ; Westcott
der; Lay Chair-   roup N Devon 1975-80; V Stoke Canon, Poltimore w
Synod Standing   om 1980; Member Doctrine Commn; Member Faith and
ion of Church

    , PHD

educ Walthamstow Hall Sevenoaks; Durham Univ; Bristol
f Resurrection   eggott Sixth Form Coll; Durham Research Student and
St James West   oll Durham; Dean St John's Coll Nottingham
Shrine of Our
c of the Holy   **t Rev Mark Santer**, MA

orough Coll; Queens' Coll Cambridge; Westcott House Th
-67; Asst C Cuddesdon 1963-67; Fellow and Dean Clare Coll
68-72); Asst Lecturer in Divinity Univ of Cambridge 1968-72;
ent Engineer   ridge 1973-81; Member Anglican-Orthodox Joint Doctrinal
31; Technical   sington 1981-87; Bp of Birmingham from 1987; Co-Chairman
mn 1971-80;   national Commn from 1983; Member Council NACRO from
neral Synod   ambridge from 1987; Queens' Coll Cambridge from 1991
4; Chairman

    ter Alan), MA

educ Merchant Taylors Sch C Northwood; Jesus Coll Cambridge;
el **Dermot**   St Nicholas Durham City 1977-80; C Emmanuel Holloway
ondon Poly and Hon C St Mary Islington 1983-89; Bps Chaplain
liffe Hall Th   9; Councillor and Chair of Planning London Borough of Islington
rist Church   Commn 1989-92; Member Panel of Chairmen General Synod
C Assembly   el Harrow from 1989; Member Church of England Evangelical
plain to Bp   ir from 1989); Member General Synod Standing Orders Ctee from
cil St John's   Executive Ctee from 1991; Member General Synod Standing Ctee
r Liturgical   tments Sub-Ctee from 1992; Chair London Diocese BSR Issues
TE Forum   ncy-in-See Ctee Regulations Working Party from 1991; Member
1991; Chair London Borough of Harrow SACRE from 1990

    hn Charles, STH, AKC

1942; *educ* Owen's Sch London; King's Coll London; St Boniface Th
Th Coll;   hael-at-Bowes 1966-70; P-in-c St Augustine Wembley Park 1970-75;
Theology   ling Ctee House of Clergy 1981-88; Area Dean Brent 1982-85; Area
r William   92; Member Panel of Chairmen 1981-84; Member Council Corpor-
ology and   80-90; TR Wood Green from 1985; Member General Synod Standing
locutor Convocation of Canterbury from 1990; Chairman Diocesan
986; Member Legal Aid Commn from 1991; Member Fees Advisory
artington   gate WCC Canberra 1991; Member ACC from 1991; Member CCBI;
1956-64;   opean Churches Prague 1992
Primary

    hbishop of, Most Rev George Leonard Carey, BD, ALCD, MTH, PHD
duc Bifrons Secondary Modern Sch Barking; London Univ; London Coll
Islington 1962-66; Lecturer Oak Hill Coll 1966-70; Lecturer St John's

Coll Nottingham 1970-75; V St Nicholas Durham 1975-82; Principal Trini
1982-87; Bp of Bath & Wells 1987-91; Abp of Canterbury from 1991

CAROL, Sister, CHN, BA
[RELIGIOUS COMMUNITIES, SOUTH] **1980-** *b* 26 Sept 1945; *educ* Merrywood Gra
King's Coll London; Relig Sister from 1970

CHATTERLEY, Mrs Dorothy, BA
[CARLISLE] **1985-** *b* 21 Dec 1932; *educ* Darwen Grammar Sch; Manchester U
CJGS Newbury 1954-56; Teacher Cumbria Education Authority 1966-86; R
man Deanery Synod; Area Sec RSCM Cumbria from 1986; Member General
Ctee and Appointments Sub-Ctee from 1990; Member Council of Corpor
House from 1989; Member CCBI and CTE from 1990

COLVEN, Canon Christopher George, BA
[LONDON] **1990-** *b* 9 June 1945; *educ* Glastonbury Sch Morden; Leeds Univ; Coll
Mirfield; C St Paul Tottenham 1968-74; C St Michael Ladbroke Grove 1974-76;
Hampstead 1976-81 (w All Souls South Hampstead 1978-81); Administrator o
Lady Walsingham 1981-87; V St Stephen South Kensington from 1987; Master
Cross from 1985; Area Dean Kensington from 1992

CRAIG, Mr Hugh Robert Morton, FIMECHE
[OXFORD] **1970-** *b* 3 Sept 1924; *educ* Highgate Sch; Bristol Univ; Chief Develop
GEC Turbine Generators Ltd 1965-78; Chief Engineer Hayward Tyler 1978
Director SPP 1981-86; Member Ch Assembly 1950-70; Member Liturgical Co
Chairman Budget Review Group 1975-77; Consulting Engineer; Member (
Standing Ctee 1965-80 and from 1985; Chairman Business Sub-Ctee 1989-
Elections Review Group from 1991; Church Commissioner from 1986; Reader

DONCASTER, Bishop of [Suffragan, Sheffield] **Rt Rev William Mich**
Persson, MA
1975-82, 1985- *b* 27 Sept 1927; *educ* Monkton Combe Sch; Oriel Coll Oxford; Wy
Coll; C Emmanuel South Croydon 1953-55; St John Tunbridge Wells 1955-58; V C
Barnet 1958-67; R Bebington 1967-79; V Knutsford w Toft 1979-82; Member B
1977-80 and 1984-90; Member Council of Wycliffe Hall from 1979; Examining C
of London 1981-82; Delegate to WCC Assembly Vancouver 1983; Member Cou
Coll Durham from 1984; Member BMU 1986-90; Member BM from 1991; Mem
Commn 1987-90; Chairman CCU from 1991; Member CCBI from 1990; Member
from 1990; Bp of Doncaster from 1982

DURHAM, Bishop of, Rt Rev David Edward Jenkins, MA, DD
1984- *b* 26 Jan 1925; *educ* St Dunstan's Coll Catford; Queen's Coll Oxford; Linco
Succentor Birmingham Cathedral 1952-54; Fellow, Chaplain and Praelector i
Queen's Coll Oxford 1954-69; Director Humanum Studies WCC 1969-73; Direc
Temple Foundation Manchester 1973-78; Prof of Theology and Head of Dept of T
Relig Studies Univ of Leeds 1979-84; Bp of Durham from 1984

ELLIS, Mrs Anne
[EXETER] **1990-** *b* 27 Aug 1936; *educ* Eccles Grammar Sch; Alsager Training Coll;
Coll of Arts; Asst Teacher and Head of Music in primary and secondary schools Lan
Notts 1964-67; Cambs 1967-82; Deputy Head Walkhampton Church of Englan
School Devon 1984-89; Housewife and Musician from 1990

ELY, Bishop of, Rt Rev Stephen Whitefield Sykes, MA
1990- *b* 1 Aug 1939; *educ* Bristol Grammar Sch; Monkton Combe Sch; St John's Coll Cambridge; Harvard Univ; Ripon Hall Th Coll; Asst Lecturer in Divinity Cambridge Univ 1964-68; Fellow and Dean St John's Coll Cambridge 1964-74; Lecturer 1968-74; Van Mildert Prof Durham Univ 1974-85; Canon Residentiary Durham Cathl 1974-85; Regius Prof of Divinity Cambridge Univ 1985-90; Bp of Ely from 1990

ETCHELLS, Dr (Dorothea) Ruth, MA, BD, DD
[DURHAM] 1985- *b* 17 Apr 1931; *educ* Merchant Taylors Sch for Girls Crosby; Liverpool Univ; London Univ; Head of English Aigburth High Sch Liverpool 1954-63; Senior Lecturer in English and Resident Tutor Chester Coll of Education 1963-68; Resident Tutor Trevelyan Coll and Lecturer in English, Univ of Durham 1968; Vice Principal Trevelyan Coll 1972-78; Senior Lecturer 1972-88; Principal St John's Coll w Cranmer Hall, Univ of Durham 1979-88; Member Doctrine Commn 1986-91; Member Crown Appts Commn from 1987

EVANS, Very Rev Thomas Eric, MA
[DEAN OF ST PAUL'S] 1970-88, 1989- *b* 1 Feb 1928; *educ* St David's Coll Lampeter; St Catherine's Coll Oxford; St Stephen's House Th Coll; C Margate 1954-58; Senior C St Peter Bournemouth 1958-62; First Director Bournemouth Samaritans 1961-62; Diocesan Youth Chaplain Gloucester 1962-69; Wing Chaplain Gloucester ATC 1963-69; Hon Chaplain Gloucester Coll of Education 1967-74; Canon Missioner 1969-75; Chairman House of Clergy Diocese of Gloucester 1975-83; Chairman Gloucester Diocesan BSR 1981-83; Adn of Cheltenham 1975-88; Chairman CCC 1981-88; Member Board of Governors of Church Commissioners from 1978; Member State Aid Working Party 1981-88; Dean of St Paul's from 1988; Director of EIG; Dean of the Order of the British Empire; Dean of the Order of St Michael and St George; Chaplain Guild of Freemen, City of London; Sub-Prelate Order of St John of Jerusalem

FIELDING, Sir Leslie, KCMG, FRSA
[CHICHESTER] 1990- *b* 29 July 1932; *educ* Queen Elizabeth Sch Barnet; Emmanuel Coll Cambridge; Sch of Oriental and African Studies London; St Anthony's Coll Oxford; HM Diplomatic Service 1956-73; Commn of the European Communities 1973-87 (Director General for External Relations 1982-87); Reader from 1981; Vice-Chancellor Sussex Univ from 1987

GAISFORD, Ven John Scott, BA, MA
[ARCHDEACON OF MACCLESFIELD] 1975- *b* 7 Oct 1934; *educ* Burnage Grammar Sch Manchester; St Chad's Coll Durham; Asst C St Hilda Audenshaw 1960-62; Asst C Bramhall 1962-65; V St Andrew Crewe 1965-86; Asst Warden of Readers for Diocese 1967-81; RD Nantwich 1974-86; Hon Canon Chester Cathl 1980-86; Chairman House of Clergy Diocesan Synod 1983-85; Adn of Macclesfield from 1986; Chairman Board of Ministry; Member Church of England Pensions Board; Vice-Chairman Housing and Residential Care Ctee; Church Commissioner from 1986; Warden of Readers from 1986; Member Redundant Churches Fund from 1989

GELDARD, Rev Peter, AKC
[CANTERBURY] 1980- *b* 21 Feb 1945; *educ* Bexhill Grammar Sch; King's Coll London; St Augustine Canterbury and Bossey, Switzerland; C Holy Trinity Sheerness 1971-78; General Sec of the Church Union 1978-87; Commissary to Bp of Matabeleland; Chairman Council of Catholic Societies; Chairman Catholic Group in General Synod; V St John the Evangelist The Brents, St Mary Magdalene and St Lawrence Davington and St Peter Oare from 1987

GRIFFITHS, Mrs Kate (Kathleen Mary), BA
[GLOUCESTER] 1985- *b* 22 Mar 1926; *educ* Alcester Grammar Sch; Durham Univ; Birmingham Univ; Principal Lecturer Coventry Coll of Education 1959-76; Housewife

GUILDFORD, Bishop of, Rt Rev Michael Edgar Adie, MA
1975- *b* 22 Nov 1929; *educ* Westminster Sch; St John's Coll Oxford; Westcott House Th Coll; Asst C St Luke, Pallion, Sunderland 1954-57; Resident Chaplain to Abp of Canterbury 1957-60; V St Mark Broomhill Sheffield 1960-69; RD Hallam 1966-69; R of Louth 1969-77; Adn of Lincoln and V Morton with Hacconby 1977-83; Bp of Guildford from 1983

GUMMER, Rt Hon John Selwyn, MP
[ST EDMUNDSBURY AND IPSWICH] **1979-** *b* 26 Nov 1939; *educ* King's Sch Rochester; Selwyn Coll Cambridge; Minister of State for Employment 1983-85; Chairman of Conservative Party 1983-1985; Minister of State for Agriculture, Fisheries and Food 1985-88; Minister for Local Government 1989; Member of Parliament for Suffolk Coastal; Minister of Agriculture, Fisheries and Food from 1989

HEIDT, Mrs Katherine Preston
[GLOUCESTER] **1985-** *b* 13 May 1943; *educ* Selwyn Sch Denton Texas; Sophie Newcombe, Tulane Univ New Orleans; Editorial Asst 'Christian World' 1978-79; President Gloucester Cursillo; National Executive WAOW; Church Union Executive

HOPE, Rev Susan, BA
[SHEFFIELD] **1990-** *b* 29 Dec 1949; *educ* St George's Sch Edinburgh; King George Vth Sch Hong Kong; St John's Coll Durham; Cranmer Hall Th Coll; Dss St Mary Boston Spa 1983-86; C St Thomas and St Margaret Brightside w Wincobank 1986-89; Dn-in-c from 1989

HOWELL, Mrs Marie Sylvester
[LONDON] **1990-** *b* 25 Oct 1928; *educ* Church of England Elementary Sch Barbados; Nurse Leavesden Hosp Watford 1956-58; part-time Forelady J L Lyons Factory 1959-75; Playgroup Leader Hammersmith Council 1976-77; Nursery Officer Maxilla Nursery Centre ILEA 1977-83; Rtd; Member Hosp Chaplaincies; Member Joint Ctee for Hosp Chaplaincy

HUGHES, Mr Michael Maximilian Ralph, MA
[SALISBURY] **1985-** *b* 19 Jan 1951; *educ* Westminster Sch; Oxford Univ; Landowner

LAIRD, Mrs Margaret Heather, BA
[EX-OFFICIO, THIRD CHURCH ESTATES COMMISSIONER] **1980-** *b* 29 Jan 1933; *educ* Truro High Sch; Westfield Coll London; King's Coll London; Divinity Mistress Grey Coat Hosp Westminster 1955-59; Divinity Mistress Newquay Grammar Sch 1959-61; Divinity Mistress St Albans High Sch 1961-62; Head of Relig Studies The Dame Alice Harpur Sch Bedford 1970-89; Third Church Estates Commissioner from 1989

LONDON, Bishop of, Rt Rev and Rt Hon David Michael Hope, BA, DPHIL, LLD
1985- *b* 14 April 1940; *educ* Queen Elizabeth Grammar Sch Wakefield; Nottingham Univ; St Stephen's House Th Coll; C St John Tue Brook Liverpool 1965-70; Chaplain Church of the Resurrection Bucharest 1967-68; V St Andrew Orford 1970-74; Principal St Stephen's House Oxford 1974-82; V All Saints Margaret Street London 1982-85; Bp of Wakefield 1985-91; Bp of London from 1991

LOVEGROVE, Mr Philip A., LLB, LLM
[ST ALBANS] **1977-** *b* 15 Aug 1937; *educ* Peter Symonds' Winchester; King's Coll London; Director Investment Bank and Industrial Companies; Church Commissioner; Chairman St Albans DBF

LOW, Mrs Sara Lindsay
[ST ALBANS] **1990-** *b* 8 June 1951; *educ* Tiffin Girls Sch; Bretton Hall Teacher Training Coll; Appeals Organiser Help the Aged 1974-76; Sales Manager Hobsons Press 1976-80; Mother; part-time TV Researcher from 1980

McCLEAN, Prof (John) David, DCL
[SHEFFIELD] **1970**- *b* 4 July 1939; *educ* Queen Elizabeth Grammar Sch Blackburn; Magdalen Coll Oxford; Barrister; Prof of Law Univ of Sheffield from 1973; Pro-Vice-Chancellor from 1991; Vice-Chairman House of Laity 1979-85; Chairman from 1985; Member Legal Advisory Commn; Lay Vice-President Diocesan Synod; Chairman Cathl Statutes Commn; Reader

MARTIN, Rev Penny (Penelope Elizabeth)
[DURHAM] **1992**- *b* 23 Oct 1944; *educ* Croydon High Sch; Cranmer Hall Durham; St John's Coll Durham; Dss Seaham w Seaham Harbour 1986-87; Parish Dn 1987-89; Parish Dn Cassop cum Quarrington from 1989

NEWCASTLE, Bishop of, Rt Rev Alec (Andrew Alexander Kenny) Graham
1975-77, 1981- *b* 7 Aug 1929; *educ* Tonbridge Sch; St John's Coll Oxford; Ely Th Coll; Asst C Hove Parish Church 1955-58; Chaplain and Lecturer in Theology Worcester Coll Oxford 1958-70; Fellow and Tutor 1960-70; Warden Lincoln Th Coll and Canon and Preb Lincoln Cathl 1970-77; Bp of Bedford 1977-81; Chairman ACCM 1984-87; Bp of Newcastle from 1981; Chairman Doctrine Commn from 1987

OSBORNE, Rev June, BA
[LONDON] **1985**- *b* 10 June 1953; *educ* Whalley Range High Sch Manchester; Manchester Univ; St John's Coll Nottingham; Wycliffe Hall Oxford; Dss St Martin's-in-the-Bullring Birmingham 1980-84; Asst Dean of Tower Hamlets and St Mark Old Ford 1984-88; TV Old Ford parishes from 1988; Member General Synod Standing Ctee; Policy Sub-Ctee; Budget Ctee; Member Dioceses Commn

PORTSMOUTH, Bishop of, Rt Rev Timothy John Bavin, MA, FRSCM, OGS
1985- *b* 17 Sept 1935; *educ* St George's Sch Windsor Castle; Brighton Coll; Worcester Coll Oxford; Cuddesdon Th Coll; Asst Pretoria Cathl 1961-64; Chaplain St Alban's Coll Pretoria 1965-68; C Uckfield and Little Horsted 1969-71; V Good Shepherd Brighton 1971-72; Dean St Mary's Cathl Johannesburg 1973-74; Bp of Johannesburg 1974-84; Bp of Portsmouth from 1985

SHEFFIELD, Bishop of, Rt Rev David Ramsay Lunn, MA
1980- *b* 17 July 1930; *educ* King's Sch Tynemouth; King's Coll Cambridge; Cuddesdon Th Coll; C Sugley 1955-59; P-in-c St Aidan Brunton Park 1959-63; Member Staff of Lincoln Th Coll 1963-70; V St George Cullercoats 1970-75; TR St George Cullercoats 1975-80; RD Tynemouth 1975-80; Bp of Sheffield from 1980

SILK, Ven (Robert) David, BA
[ARCHDEACON OF LEICESTER] **1970**- *b* 23 Aug 1936; *educ* Gillingham Grammar Sch; Exeter Univ; St Stephen House Th Coll; C St Barnabas Gillingham 1959-63; C Holy Redeemer Lamorbey 1963-69; P-in-c The Good Shepherd Blackfen 1967-69; R Swanscombe 1969-75; R St George Beckenham 1975-80; TR Holy Spirit Leicester 1982-88; Member Liturgical Commn 1976-91; Adn of Leicester from 1980; Prolocutor Lower House Convocation of Canterbury from 1980; Chairman Leicestershire Council of Faiths from 1986; Moderator Churches' Commn for Inter-Faith Relations (formerly CRPOF) from 1990

SOUTHWARK, Bishop of, Rt Rev Dr Roy (Robert Kerr) Williamson
1979- *b* 18 Dec 1932; *educ* Elmgrove Sch Belfast; Oak Hill Th Coll; Asst C All Saints Crowborough 1963-66; V Hyson Green Nottingham 1966-71; V St Ann w Emmanuel Nottingham 1971-76; V Bramcote 1976-79; Adn of Nottingham 1978-84; Bp of Bradford 1984-91; Bp of Southwark from 1991

STANLEY, Canon John
[LIVERPOOL] **1973**- *b* 20 May 1931; *educ* Birkenhead Sch; Tyndale Hall Th Coll; C All Saints

Preston 1956-60; C St Mark St Helens 1960-63; V St Cuthbert Everton 1963-70; P-in-c St Saviour 1969-70; V St Saviour w St Cuthbert 1970-74; Chairman Diocesan House of Clergy 1979-85; Member BCC 1984-87; V Huyton from 1974; Area Dean Huyton from 1989; Church Commissioners from 1983; Board of Governors from 1989; Hon Canon Liverpool Cathl from 1987; Trustee Church Urban Fund from 1987; Prolocutor York Convocation from 1990

WILLIAMS, Mrs Shirley-Ann, LRAM, LLAM
[EXETER] **1985-** *b* 15 May 1933; *educ* Barr's Hill Sch Coventry; Leeds Univ; part-time Tutor in Speech and Drama, Public Speaking and Communication Skills; Member Diocesan Pastoral Ctee; Member Bps Council and Standing Ctee; Chairman Diocesan Board of Patronage; Member Diocesan Children and Young People's Ctee; Chairman Ecumenical Ctee Churches of Devon Stand (Devon County Show); Member Diocesan Lay Training Team; Member Diocesan Adult Training Ctee; Chairman Diocesan House of Laity from 1982; Member Community Council of Devon Executive Ctee and Chairman Health and Welfare Ctee; Deanery Lay Chairman; Diocesan Co-ordinator Ecumenical Decade of Churches in Solidarity with Women

YORK, Archbishop of, Most Rev and Rt Hon John Stapylton Habgood, PHD, DD
1973- *b* 23 June 1927; *educ* Eton; King's Coll Cambridge; Cuddesdon Th Coll; C St Mary Abbots Kensington 1954-56; Vice-Principal Westcott House Th Coll 1956-62; R St John Jedburgh 1962-67; Principal The Queen's Coll Birmingham 1967-73; Bp of Durham 1973-83; Abp of York from 1983

THE ORDINATION OF WOMEN
IN THE ANGLICAN COMMUNION

The ordination of women began with a wartime emergency for pastoral needs. The Rev Li Tim Oi was priested in 1944 by Bishop R. O. Hall of Hong Kong in a small southern China city. That decision caused much controversy, and Li Tim Oi ceased to act a priest. The 1968 Lambeth Conference asked the member churches to study the question of the ordination of women to the priesthood and to report its findings to the Anglican Consultative Council. Very little had been received by way of response before the ACC, at its first meeting in 1971, resolved by 24 votes to 22 that if a bishop (acting with the approval of his Province) ordained a woman to the priesthood 'his action will be acceptable to this Council; and that this Council will use its good offices to encourage all Provinces of the Anglican Communion to continue in communion with these dioceses'. Thus in 1971 the first two legal ordinations were held in Hong Kong. What next followed were illegal ordinations, 'the Philadelphia 11' in the USA in 1976, later regularised by the General Convention when the Province of the USA adopted the legislation to ordain women to all orders.

Sixteen of the thirty Provinces of the Communion ordain women to the diaconate with the total number being 1,962. Most of these, it is believed, would seek ordination as priests: however in places such as the USA and Canada there are also 'permanent deacons', both male and female. Fifteen Provinces have ordained women to the priesthood within their boundaries. Not all were ordained under provincial legislation: the Archdiocese of Perth in Australia went ahead with ordinations to the priesthood while provincial legislation, passed in November 1992, was still pending. Southern Africa, a largely Anglo-Catholic province, also recently approved the ordination of women to the priesthood, and the first ordinations took place there in September 1992. It is estimated that nearly 1,400 women serve as priests in the Anglican Communion. Of these over one thousand are in the Episcopal Church of the United States of America (ECUSA). Apart from Canada (158), New Zealand (120) and Uganda (36), no other Anglican Church had more than ten women priests in September 1992.

The Anglican Communion, as of December 1992, has one diocesan bishop, in New Zealand, an English woman, Penelope Jamieson, and two suffragan bishops in the USA: Barbara Harris, who was the first woman to be consecrated a bishop in the Communion, and Jane Dixon, who was consecrated suffragan bishop of Washington DC in November 1992.

THE ORDINATION OF WOMEN AND THE GENERAL SYNOD OF THE CHURCH OF ENGLAND

HISTORICAL BACKGROUND

1975   Motion that 'There are no fundamental objections to the ordination of women to the priesthood' *carried*: *For* 255 *Against* 180. Motion to remove 'legal and other barriers' *lost*.

1978   Motion to remove legal barriers lost (in the House of Clergy only).

1984   *November*
General Synod agrees to 'bring forward legislation to permit ordination of women to the priesthood'.

1985   *July*
Legislation to ordain women as deacons received Final Approval.

1986   *July*
Motion to allow women priests from overseas Anglican provinces to officiate in England. Needed two-thirds majority in each of the three houses. *Lost.*
Report outlining scope of the legislation *received*. The matter was referred to the Bishops to produce a Report.

1987   *February*
First Report from the House of Bishops (with promise of further reflection) *received*. Motion asking Standing Committee to prepare draft legislation *carried* as follows:

	AYES	NOES
Bishops	32	8
Clergy	135	70
Laity	150	67

1987   First women deacons ordained (i.e. in Holy Orders).

1988   *July*
Second Report from the House of Bishops *received*. Draft legislation to enable women to be ordained to the priesthood was generally approved and sent to a Revision Committee.

	AYES	NOES
Bishops	28	21
Clergy	137	102
Laity	134	93

Draft financial provision for stipendiary church workers to resign on 'conscience' grounds if women were ordained was also generally approved and referred to the Revision Committee.

1989   *June*
Report of the Revision Committee on the legislation and the House of Bishops' proposed code of practice were published.

1989   *November*
Revised legislation was amended and carried:

	AYES	NOES
Bishops	30	17
Clergy	149	85
Laity	144	78

1990   Draft legislation for the Ordination of Women to the Priesthood was referred to the Diocesan Synods under Article 8 of the constitution of the General Synod of the Church of England. Under Article 8, the General Synod could only proceed towards the Final Approval stage for this legislation if a majority of the 44 Diocesan Synods indicated their approval. Such a majority (38 dioceses) indicated their approval by majority votes in both their Diocesan House of Clergy and Diocesan House of Laity.

1992   *February*
General Synod debated the Standing Committee report on the Article 8 reference to the Dioceses.

Final Drafting was completed.

1992   *June*
House of Bishops debated the final draft of the legislation in accordance with Article 7 of the Constitution and passed it on unaltered.

July
The legislation was 'claimed' for debate in the separate Houses of the Convocations of Canterbury and York and the House of Laity of the General Synod.

(The Convocations of Canterbury and York consist of the Upper House – Archbishop, Bishops and elected Suffragan Bishops of the Province – and Lower House – ex officio and elected members of the clergy of the Province. Combined, the four Houses of Convocation form the House of Bishops and House of Clergy of the General Synod.)
On a simple majority it was approved in all four houses of Convocation and in the House of Laity.

TOTALS AND PERCENTAGES FOR THE MEASURE
The figures for Bishops and Clergy are the figures for Canterbury and York combined.

Bishops	FOR	31	70.45%	AGAINST	13	29.55%
Clergy	FOR	164	68.91%	AGAINST	74	31.09%
Laity	FOR	148	61.41%	AGAINST	93	38.59%

NOVEMBER 1992: FINAL APPROVAL

On Wednesday 11 November 1992, the General Synod passed, by a two-thirds majority in all three Houses, the Priests (Ordination of Women) Measure. The voting was as follows: House of Bishops, 39 Ayes, 13 Noes – 75%; House of Clergy, 176 Ayes, 74 Noes –70.4%; and the House of Laity, 169 Ayes, 82 Noes – 67.3%

The Synod also passed by a simple majority in each House the Ordination of Women (Financial Provisions) Measure. Voting was as follows: House of Bishops, 35 Ayes, 0 Noes; House of Clergy, 225 Ayes, 7 Noes; House of Laity, 220 Ayes, 11 Noes. This measure provides, subject to certain conditions, financial support for full-time ordained clergy, deaconesses and licensed lay workers who, following the promulgation of the relevant canon, resign on the grounds that they are opposed to the ordination of women as priests.

The legislation has now been committed to the Legislative Committee of the General Synod for onward reference to the Ecclesiastical Committee which has 30 members representing equally both Houses of Parliament. If this committee deems the legislation 'expedient', it will be laid before both Houses for debate and approval. The legislation may not be amended. Assuming the legislation is approved by both Houses, the Royal Assent will follow, hopefully in the summer. Depending on the Parliamentary timetable, the associated Canons will be promulged at the next convenient meeting of Synod. This could be in November 1993 or, failing this, July 1994. (From 1994 the Synod will meet only twice a year, in July and late November.) Ordinations can take place as soon as the Canons have been promulged.

Under the legislation a diocesan bishop opposed to women priests who is in office at the date of the promulgation of the canon may make any or all of the following declarations: that a woman priest may not be ordained in the diocese; may not be an incumbent, priest-in-charge or team vicar; may not be licensed to officiate. Such a declaration, where made, will remain in force until six months after a successor takes up office. However, a woman priest may officiate in a parish at the invitation of the parish priest, without reference to the bishop, for a period of not more than seven days in any period of three months.

A Parochial Church Council also may pass a resolution stating it would not accept a woman president at Holy Communion, nor to pronounce Absolution; and it would not accept a woman as incumbent, priest-in-charge or team vicar.

The House of Bishops is considering how best to operate the Code of Practice linked to the new legislation in ways which will underpin the House's intention to continue to provide episcopal oversight and pastoral care for all members of the Church. In his presidential address to the November Synod, the Archbishop of Canterbury stressed there should be no discrimination in selection against those opposed to the ordination of women to the priesthood. The House of Bishops stood by the introduction to the draft Code of Practice prepared by the House which states: 'Christian charity and the exercise of true pastoral care require that careful provision be made to respect as far as possible' the position of those who remain opposed to the legislation. He concluded: 'There is certainly no question of those who continue to doubt the theological justification for the priesting of women having any less place within our Church.'